Dirt + Vine = Wine

Dirt + Vine = Wine

How Grape Growers Transformed Three Miles of Terrior and Shaped a Pinot Noir Revolution

By Kerry McDaniel Boenisch

ISBN: 1511584076
ISBN-13: 9781511584074

Terrier in the Vineyard Publishing
P.O. Box 383
Dundee, Oregon 97115

Dedication:

For all the Oregon wine growers, a heartfelt thank you for all those years of dedication to the dream.

In honor of the enduring spirit of Loie Maresh, who encouraged me to write these stories and spent many hours talking to me about them. Unfortunately this book was published after the death of another vineyard pioneer, Arthur Weber, who with his wife Vivian also supported me throughout the writing process, as well as Paige Fuqua. Julia and Gerry were always ready with a glass of wine and words of support. Vivian, Jim Maresh, John Davidson, Gary Fuqua and Dick Erath, thanks for letting me be part of the geezers club for one entertaining lunch. And thanks for sharing the memories of our 1970s neighborhood Julia and Bill Wayne.

With this publication I also honor all the people in the Oregon wine industry who contribute to the success of the industry on a daily basis working pouring in tasting rooms, driving tractors and tying vines in vineyards.

I also dedicate this book to my remarkable, beloved parents, husband and children.

Prologue

These are stories about what Dundee vineyard life was like for grape growers in the Worden Hill neighborhood during the 1970s and 1980s. It is a revised and updated edition of my book "Vineyard Memoirs" and will reflect that changes in the industry since it was published in 2004.

The following account is based on my personal recollections. I have also included interviews that I conducted with other families who planted vineyards in the Worden Hill Road community. I think that if ten different people attend one party, chances are you'll have ten slightly different recollections of the same event. Therefore, I take all responsibility for my own recollections, be what they may, and hope you enjoy my perspective.

It was a marvelous and gut-wrenching experience. It was also an experience that became part of my soul. This story is not a comprehensive history of the Oregon wine industry, although at first I thought it might be. Instead, it is an attempt to share a time and a place in history. I have slowly been collecting my own recollections on the back of napkins and scrap paper, and occasionally interviewing the other people who were there in hopes that one day I would produce a monumental tome to the history of Oregon wine. Instead, I wrote about our neighborhood vineyards.

In 1973, my parents Jim and Donna Jean McDaniel, purchased three separate acreages in the Red Hills above Dundee, Oregon. We planted vineyards on all three. The biggest parcel consisted of fifteen acres of an old prune orchard and a field filled with blackberries. After we cleared the land, we planted a vineyard and built a house. Today that house and vineyard is called Torii Mor Winery. For the 15 years that we lived and worked there it was known as McDaniel Vineyards, and we, along with the other grape growers in the neighborhood, helped establish the Oregon wine industry.

I am sharing a compilation of my interviews and my own story with you now. I hope that I have captured the spirit of the adventure we all felt and that you are inspired to pursue your own dreams. If we can get people from all over the world to visit our little one-stoplight town, I'm convinced anything is possible.

SECTION ONE: The growth of the Oregon Wine industry coincides with rise in the tourism, restaurant and hotel industry

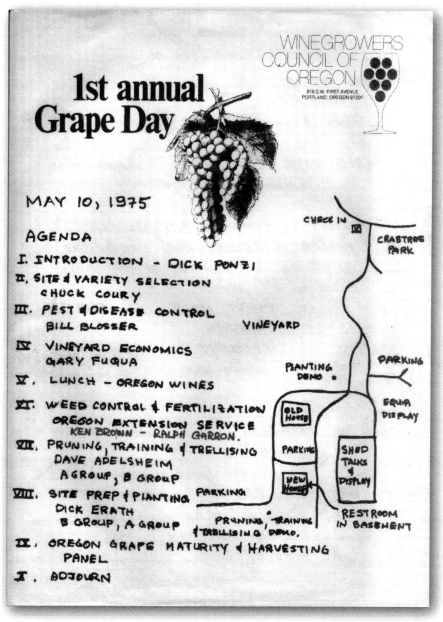

Winegrowers Council of Oregon First Annual Grape Day, 1975

In the early 1960's, University of California at Davis in Sacramento, an area rich in agricultural and wine growing history, began to offer classes in winemaking and enology. Recent UC graduates, including Charles Coury, Bill Fuller, David Lett and Dick Erath, began to look for places to establish themselves and use their academic training. The beginning of a new interest in winemaking began concurrently with a very similar emergence of the industry in California. For various reasons, these winemaker's and others soon after them choose Oregon as their ideal locale to establish wineries. The few Oregon vineyards and wineries that were already established in the 1960's included Honeywood and Hillcrest Winery.

By 1978, there were approximately 35 Vineyards and wineries in northern and southern Oregon.

"They were a diverse lot," said Bessie Archibald, Archibald Vineyards. "In fact, you've never seen such diversity in one room before."

This group of people organized a very loosely defined organization called the Oregon Winegrowers Association. The winegrowers were divided by locale into two regions: north and south.

Southern Oregon wine industry

While grape growers were just beginning to plant in the Dundee Hills in the late 1960s, grape growers in the southern part of the state were expanding on a few already established wineries.

Communication between both groups was still cohesive, although the growers were divided by different grape growing climates. Eventually, the rapid expansion of the industry in the northern Willamette Valley and the slower, yet still quality growth of the southern Oregon wineries, created divisions that still exist today. They were divided by the miles and by the sizes of their respective industries, yet they were still united in their goal to produce quality Oregon wine.

The middle part of the state, Roseburg and Douglas County, was slightly different climate than the northern Oregon Willamette Valley. The far southern region, including Grants Pass, differed in climate temperatures variation from the Willamette Valley by as much as a ten degree difference during the same season. Gewurtraminer, Tempranillo and Cabernet Sauvignon were hardier in the southern regions.

However, in the beginning of the modern Oregon wine industry (1965 and later) wineries in the Southern region played a significant part beginning with founding winemaker Richard Sommers of Hillcrest Vineyards. The Doerner family, a 100 year-old farming family in Roseburg, where among some of the first, along with Honeywood, to make commercial wine in the state after prohibition. Valley View Winery was established by the Wisnovsky family in 1976. Tualatin Valley winemaker Bill Fuller crafted their first vintage. Doyle Hinman, who currently owns DW Cellars in Eugene, planted five acres of grapes in 1972 and established his commercial vineyard in 1979. He was also one of the first organizers of the Oregon Wine Board Export Program, and was the first Oregon winemaker to export bulk Pinot Noir to Sweden. Scott Henry and his wife Sylvia of Henry Estate planted their first 12 acres with the help of their children in the Umpqua region in 1972. Henry was an aeronautical engineer who had returned to the Umpqua Valley where he was raised. He also developed the Scott Henry Trellis System for vines, which he promotes in the international marketplace.

Douglas County Public Meeting 1971:

On February 9, 1971, a group of wine growers from both northern and southern Oregon gathered at a public meeting organized by David Passon, an Oregon horticulture extension agent. Charles Coury, David Lett, Dick Erath, Ray Doerner and Richard Sommers were present at the seminar, whose minutes were titled "Prospects of a Grape and Wine Industry for Oregon."

The seminar speeches were prophetic.

Extension Agent David Passon greeted the crowd with this introduction:

"As you all know grape production and the prospect of a wine industry in Western Oregon have created a gold rush atmosphere throughout the western states in recent months," said Passon.

Panel discussion ensued at the meeting, beginning with Richard Sommer:

"I am Richard Sommer, owner of Hillcrest Vineyard. I have twenty acres located ten miles N.W. of Roseburg, Oregon. If you want to produce a quality wine you have to have four things going for you. You have to have the right variety, climate, soil and winemaking. If one of these items is missing from the program you will not come out with extraordinary wine. I started in 1961 with a mother block of eight varieties going from Gewürztraminer, Chardonnay, Cabernet Sauvignon, Sauvignon blanc, White Riesling and Pinot noir. I don't know if we are Burgundy or Bordeaux or what so we still have to keep plugging along to see which one we stick to, two or three varieties. I'd like to go with one variety, it would probably be better than a whole mess of them."

The next person on the panel was David Lett:

"My name is David Lett. I operate Eyrie Vineyards in the Dundee Hills near McMinnville. I am a graduate of U.C. at Davis in Viticulture and have been growing grapes in the Willamette Valley since 1965 concentrating on viniferas. I am supposed to give the view from Yamhill County and I think I will do it for the Northwest corner, which includes Washington and Yamhill counties. I have fifteen acres planted, Dick Erath with fifteen and Chuck Coury with twenty up in Washington County. I think I speak for all three of us, we feel that Oregon has a unique potential on this entire planet for vinifera varieties and we want to see it done well."

Lett commented that he was focusing on three particular grapes that he felt were well suited for the environment: Pinot noir, Chardonnay and Riesling.

A lengthy discussion ensued about the ripening time, sugar and acid content of wine grapes:

Chuck Coury comments: "A lot of our thinking is based on California. Taking those sugars you are talking about (sic), I'd consider it a damn fine Pinot noir and it would taste good too. I think we are going to have to create our own concept and criteria for what good quality is. Grapes here are more similar to Europe than California. There is an entirely different situation in Oregon and we are going to have to start directing our thinking to Oregon, not California. We can use guidelines from California and their certified cuttings."

The modern era:

The industry pioneers of the 1970s established a foundation for both the modern Oregon wine industry and the local travel and recreation industry. Gourmet restaurants began to flourish as interest in food and wine pairing grew. Tourism to the state increased as wineries attracted vacationers from all over the world. The hotel and bed and breakfast industry thrived with new patrons.

Ken Wright of Ken Wright Cellars was featured in the May 2015 cover of the Wine Spectator. Many other Oregon winemakers have been featured in The Wine Spectator, Wines and Vines, and countless other media outlets nationally and internationally.

Joan and Ken Austin and their family, founders of ADEC dental equipment, founded the Forbes four-star rated Allison Hotel in Newberg in 2009.

The Austin family created the only hotel of it's kind in Oregon and simultaneously created a place for the Oregon Wine Industry to compete in an international wine destination system stretching from Bordeaux to Napa. The hotel features a restaurant, spa and pool with lavish artwork and a vineyard. It has four levels, 77 deluxe guest rooms and 8 custom suites. The most expensive treatment at the in-house luxury spa is $740 for the "ever-after" treatment package.

In the modern era, women winemakers like Louisa Ponzi, Patricia Green and Lynn Penner-Ash have made prominent places for themselves, as well as Wynne Peterson-Nedry, daughter of Chehalem Winery founder Harry Nedry and Judy Peterson-Nedry. The second and third generation of children of grape growers are now involved in the once fledgling industry.

Tom Huggins, founder of Eola Hills Winery in Rickreal, harvested his first vintage in 1986 and established one of the first custom crush facilities in the state. Huggins developed a private label crushing program to serve the clients of the burgeoning hotel, restaurant and corporate industries interested in local wines. Eola Hills continues to operate it's crush facility and several tasting rooms in the region.

Laurent Montalieu, co-founder of NW Wine Company, operates one of the largest custom crush companies in the state. In 2007 the company bought and craft Pinot noir from Hyland Vineyards in the McMinnville AVA coast range foothills, a historic vineyard planted in 1971.

Red Hills Market, a restaurant that owner's Jody and Michelle Kropf founded in 2011, features a casual wine country atmosphere and has become a wine country destination.

Jody is a local Oregonian and Michelle was raised in Napa. They combined their love of local food and wine and created an extremely popular restaurant menu featuring craft sandwiches, wood-fired pizza, soups and salads; as well as local micro-brews on tap and of course a wall of local wines. Picnics are available to go. The deli cases display a selection of cheeses, meats and house-made salads and feature local products like Briar Rose chèvre, a Dundee cheese company.

A bocce ball court and outdoor seating add to the casual ambience.

"We are conscious and responsible in our buying practices, striving to source natural, local and pesticide free products when possible" is listed on the bottom of the menu.

The recent developments in the thriving restaurant and hotel industry are a sharp contrast to the tourism industry in the 1980s.

David Bergen of Tina's restaurant in Dundee remembers when they had about fifteen Oregon wines that they offered, which included Knudsen Erath, Eyrie, Bethel Heights, Arterberry, Tualatin, Hinman and Lange. Their 2015 wine lists includes over 200 wines.

"The industry was just beginning to come together. I actually had more white wines than reds. Some were spectacular. A few were awful," said Bergen.

He noted that the second generation of wine makers added depth and expertise to the rapidly growing industry - John Paul of Cameron Winery, Rollin Soles of Argyle Winery and Ken Wright of Ken Wright Cellars.

Bergen worked in the restaurant industry in Portland before his move to Dundee in 1988 to the Red Hills. He remembers working at 2601 Vaughn Street Restaurant during some of the first winemaker dinners, which were special events featuring winemakers David Lett and Myron Redford.

Bergen formed the successful Ron Paul Charcuterie in N.W. Portland before he and his wife Tina opened Tina's in 1991.

"We focused on Oregon wines from the beginning. They had world-class potential," said Bergen.

Dundee is now a mecca for fine dining. The town that used to have a truck-stop and a drive-in hamburger restaurant now features Tina's, Ponzi's Dundee Bistro, The Red Hills restaurant,

Before the influx of new restaurants in the 1990s, one convenience store, Alfie's French restaurant, preceded by the Khyber, an Afghan restaurant, and Alice's Restaurant were the sole dining options. Eventually, John's Truck Stop diner, Pinot Pete's restaurant opened and garnered dedicated clientele.

A second generation followed the growers and winemakers of the 1970s. In the 1980s, new winery owners established a larger and more commercialized industry that began to expand rapidly into the restaurant, grocery and international wine industry. The larger wineries of the eighties were owned and operated with significant financial backing or by corporations. These wineries created tremendous growth for industry.

The division between those who grew grapes and those who grew grapes and operated a commercial winery began to grow. Growers had to make choices about what they wanted from their vineyard. They could choose to operate as a grower and sell their grapes to a winery or start a commercial winery and operate a tasting room. They were faced with formidable choices.

Thus, larger wineries also signified a change in winery operations. In the early 1980s, Paul Hart and his wife Jan Jacobsen established their winery north of Newberg on 99w and Rex Hill. They also formed Oregon Vineyard Management Company, which was the first of its kind in the area. The company managed vineyards, year round, with the rights to buy your harvest at the end of the year or other contractual terms.

Medici vineyards, Archibald, Weber and Maresh all used the service for part or all of their vineyards. Rex Hill produced the wine with the vineyard designate: Maresh vineyards, 88 Pinot noir, etc.

This service enabled the vineyard owners to continue to own and operate their vineyards. Rex Hill promoted these vineyards along with their own and soon these growers received national and international recognition with the growing distribution and popularity of Rex Hill wines.

No one had a computer. Many of the owners did the books in ledgers or along with the household budget. Incoming money originally only came from two sources, selling their tonnage or selling their wine. Neither source was dependable for primary income to support a family.

The third wave of wineries heralded from international corporations and winemakers from France, Germany and Australia.

Oregon currently has spectacular wineries on a scale to match other wine regions internationally.

The owner's of the King Estate winery own eight-hundred and twenty acres and built their winery in the grand style of a European chateau. It has a propagating and grapevine grafting facility, winemaking equipment, vineyards and nursery. Inside the facility are plush eating accommodations.

In 2003 Chemekata Community College in Salem, Oregon, opened the Northwest Viticultural Center to train students for the wine industry. The second viticultural center serving Southern Oregon opened the same decade. In 2015, the program supporters are now expanding viticultural training centers to community college locations throughout Oregon.

Since 1983, the McMenamin brothers continue to build a historic hotel and movie theater empire featuring local beer, cider and wine in the Pacific Northwest. The brothers were among the first to promote local wines in their pubs alongside their micro-brewed beers. They also craft wine in their Edgefield Winery.

The grape growers had succeeded.

*Reprinted from Oregon Wine Press, May 2015, by Kerry McDaniel Boenisch

DUNDEE VITICULTURISTS:
THE FIRST WINEGROWERS ON WORDEN HILL ROAD

"Del vino vine l'uva, dall'uva il vino, dal vino un sogno.
From the vine came the grape, from the grape came the wine, from the wine a dream...,"

SONG WRITTEN BY PAUL CUNNINGHAM AND LEONARD WHITCUP, 1954.

"For some, the discovery carries an aura of gold rush fever that once grasped the imaginations of early day prospectors. The less optimistic consider it nothing more than a real estate promotions scheme. Between these two extremes is a handful of dedicated viticulturists (wine grape growers) risking their capitol and futures on the promise that Oregon is capable of producing and establishing a competitive market for wine grapes. Joining the viticulturists, and perhaps outnumbering them, are part-time growers going into the grape business as a sideline to full-time jobs or professions in other areas," excerpted from Wine Industry Grows in Oregon, by Oregon State Press staff, 1972.

David Lett, the founder of Eyrie Vineyards, appeared on the doorstep of Jim McDaniel's McMinnville granary in 1970. He asked McDaniel if he could buy a building from him near the current site of the Granary District to make wine. McDaniel obliged and sold him a small outbuilding on Alpine Avenue.

Helping Lett make his first vintage in 1970 inspired McDaniel to purchase a fifteen acre vineyard in the Dundee Red Hills Worden Hill Road neighborhood in 1972, where he built a family home and established McDaniel Vineyards, now Torii Mor Winery.

When Rollin Soles, founder of Argyle and Roco Winery, arrived in Oregon in 1985, he was introduced to McDaniel by Allen Holstein, who was then working as the vineyard manager at Knudsen-Erath. He was also managing McDaniel's vineyard. Soles lived at the McDaniel's house that fall and made wine in the basement. It didn't seem unusual to McDaniel at the time, he valued the help from the young men who would eventually become luminaries in the Oregon wine industry.

Throughout the two decades, more people bought land and planted vineyards in the three mile radius of Worden Hill and Fairview roads. By 1980 there were 10 operating vineyards in the neighborhood.

The early winemaking community in the neighboring Yamhill, Washington and Polk County hillsides also included Adelsheim, Amity Vineyards, Bethel Heights, Honeywood, Sokol-Blosser, Ponzi, Coury/Hillcrest, Shafer, Elk Cove, Tualatin, Oak Knoll, Elk Cove and others albeit one distinct difference - the Worden Hill Road grape growers grew and sold most of their tonnage for wineries to commercially produce.

They are part of the group of Oregon pioneer viticulturists, the grape growers, the planters of the vine. The vine came before the wine.

The story of the grape growers living the Worden Hill neighborhood began with a man on a tractor farming his prune, cherry and hazelnut orchards. His name was Jim Maresh. He and his wife, Loie, purchased their first acreage in 1959.

The Maresh family, originally from Wisconsin, lived with their five children on their bucolic country farm until one day in 1969, when a man drove up their driveway in an old beat up BMW.

"I've looked all over the West Coast for a great viticulture site and I think you're sitting on it," said Dick Erath, after he stepped out of the car and knocked on Maresh's door.

The only vineyard in Yamhill County at the time was David Lett's.

Erath asked Maresh if he was interested in wine grapes.

Maresh replied, "Well, I've tried everything else."

Erath suggested that they build a greenhouse on Maresh's property. He also proposed that they could get cuttings from Wente Nursery in California to propagate root stock for planting vineyards on both of their properties. Erath also suggested using root stock from Charles Coury's nursery at Coury's recently established Forest Grove winery, Laurel Ridge. Maresh agreed to the proposition. Erath propagated grapes with Maresh for years after their first meeting while he was simultaneously establishing Knudsen-Erath a mile north of the Maresh Farm on Worden Hill Road. Their friendship has endured for forty-four years.

After building the greenhouse, Maresh and his wife Loie obliged Dick and planted a vineyard. They later renovated their red barn for a tasting room and crossed their fingers that grapes would sell as well as the cherry and hazelnuts they were previously farming.

This community of viticulturists, who were generally trained to be anything but grape growers, planted grapes until a network of vineyards covered the hillsides where hazelnut orchards once dominated the landscape. They joined the Maresh and Erath family and formed a diverse neighborhood community united by the desire to grow wine grapes.

The group included Bill Archibald and Gary Fuqua, the first two growers in the neighborhood after Maresh and Erath to plant grapes, followed by Jim McDaniel. Fuqua and McDaniel were the only native Oregonians. Arthur and Vivian Weber planted Weber Vineyards. John Bauer planted a vineyard currently owned by Winderlea Winery. Bill and Julia Wayne planted Abbey Ridge Vineyard, and later became affiliated with winemaker John Paul/Cameron Winery. Tom Saucy planted the vineyard now owned by Julia Staigers and Gerard Koschal of Crumbled Rock, who along with Don and Wendy Lange joined the Dundee Hills neighborhood in 1987.

The growers helped each other in various ways. They loaned tractors for tilling and debated effective bird deterrents. They celebrated harvest, bud break and anything else they could think of to keep themselves forging ahead into the unknown, then debated some more. They learned from each other's mistakes and successes.

During the early growing era, before the advent of prolific commercial wineries, many of these families grew grapes and sold their tonnage to a fledgling group of local winemakers including Dick Erath, Myron Redford and David Adelsheim, along with Elk Cove Vineyard owners Pat and Joe Campbell.

Visits to neighborhood parties and early Oregon winegrower association meetings that included Dick and Nancy Ponzi, Susan and Bill Sokol-Blosser, David and Diana Lett and Shirley and Charles Coury, who planted the famous Coury Clone, were common.

Many of the early growers planted his cuttings, which were primarily the Pommard Clone, mixed with his infamous 'Coury Clone,' which years later he admitted came from Alsace in his suitcase.

Charles Coury, David Lett and Bill Fuller all attended the University of California/Davis in the early 1960s to study viticulture. Erath also attended UC/Davis in the late 1960s. They formed a competitive alliance and had heated conversations about the ideal cool climate growing locale for wine grapes. They also debated early bottling and labeling laws with fervor.

In 1976 Dan Berger, a reporter for the Salem Statesman, interviewed Dick Erath on the topic of bottling and labeling regulations:

"We had a lot of ideas," said Dick Erath of Erath Vineyards, "But no one agreed with anyone else about what was the best thing. Getting two winemakers to agree on anything is like trying to get 100 cats in a sack."

Eventually David Adelsheim negotiated and lead the legislation for labeling regulations.

Dick Erath sold nursery rootstock besides buying many of the grapes from the winegrowers in his neighborhood at their winery Knudsen-Erath. He wrote in an Erath Nursery newsletter advertising grape cutting stock dated September 1977 and listed 'dormant bare root plants .50 cents each, in bundles of 50.'

Erath crafted Pinot noir, Chardonnay and Riesling (for his German father). He also made a wine he named 'Coastal Mist'. The sweet blend appealed to the palates of a burgeoning crowd of Oregon wine drinking enthusiasts who gradually had begun to frequent the Knudsen-Erath tasting room Dick constructed in the basement garage of his home. The same basement room is still currently in use by Chateau St. Michelle.

"Kina Erath and I opened the garage door of the tasting room the first day and wondered if people would show up," said Martha Maresh, who helped run the fledgling Knudsen-Erath tasting room in the early 1970s.

Planting, growing and maintaining a vineyard was hard work for the growers and the weather was unpredictable. The harvests were grueling. They hoped they were lucky enough to sell their young Pinot noir and Chardonnay grapes to a winery to cover operating costs.

Gary Fuqua, who planted Fuqua Vineyards in 1972, was an economist for Bonneville Power Administration during the day and came home to manage the vineyard after work. He detailed startup vineyard costs for local growers in his 1972 Vineyard Establishment Costs, Willamette Valley, Oregon document:

"Both ends of the cost spectrum were analyzed to try to determine what a grower might expect to pay at the low end and the high end on a per acre basis. The low-end of price per acre is $1200 and the high end is $2,000. Labor cost is $3 an hour. The interest rate for borrowing money from the bank is 9%. Vineyard harvest costs include picking, at 4 tons an acre for $50 a ton," wrote Fuqua.

Even after three decades the grower's clearly remember their first harvests:

Bill Wayne and his wife Julia planted their vineyard, Abbey Ridge in 1977. They have been growers with Cameron Winery since John Paul formed the winery in 1984, along with Marc Dochez and Shawna Archibald.

"Our first harvest happened in conjunction with the 1978 Mt. St. Helens eruption. Our shoulders were covered with fine gray ash but we picked fifteen boxes of grapes with Marc and Shawna," said Wayne.

Julia Staigers and Gerard Koschal, who grew grapes in their vineyard Juliard before they opened Crumbled Rock Winery, recalled their early attempt to sell their Riesling grapes in 1988:

"We put several boxes of freshly harvested grapes at the top of our driveway on Worden Hill Road with a handwritten sign advertising the grapes for $250 a ton. We taped the sign on the boxes and waited. Ironically the person who stopped to inquire about buying the grapes was a winemaker, Bill Heron from Rogue River Winery in Southern Oregon. He came back with his truck and took all the boxes," said Julia.

The couple sold their next harvest to Heron and focused on Willamette Valley wineries to sell their grapes to after their roadside marketing attempt. Throughout the years they established vineyard contracts with Erath, Amity and many others.

Their significance of these fledgling vineyards was also noticed internationally. Significant, simultaneous land purchases by wine luminaries occurred in 1986 and 1987. The purchases brought national and international interest to the small segment of Oregon winegrowers. Domaine Drouhin purchased 90 acres of vineyard land in the Red Hills near Sokol Blosser. In the town of Dundee, Argyle Winery was founded by Rollin Soles, along with partner Brian Crosier, who was a partial owner of Petaluma Winery in Australia. Additionally, Robert Parker, an influential wine writer from Maryland who established the groundbreaking Wine Advocate publication, decided to join the Oregon wine industry. He partnered with his brother in law, Michael Etzel, and purchased an 88 acre pig farm in the Ribbon Ridge appellation where they established Beaux Freres. Also in 1987 Joe Dobbes of Dobbes Winery, which would eventually be a significant producer for the Dundee Hills, became Cellar Master at Elk Cove Vineyards.

The advent of vineyards created a need for vineyard managers. Along with Allen Holstein, Joel Meyers, Mark Benoit and John Davidson, who founded Walnut City Wineworks, began working in the industry in the 1980s.

The Maresh family has produced grapes through all the changes in the industry. Jim's grandson Jimmy is the third generation to grow grapes. His label Arterberry-Maresh is named after his deceased father, Fred Arterberry Jr., who was the first Oregon winemaker to produce sparkling wine and cider in 1980, along with his wife Martha Maresh. Throughout the 1980s the pair produced 600 cases of sparkling wine a year. The other four early industry sparkling winemakers included Dick Erath, Gerard Rottiers of Chateau Benoit Winery, Robert Hudson of Ellendale Vineyards and Rich Cushman of Laurel Ridge Winery.

Jim Maresh was inducted into the Ponzi wine walk hall of fame in November of 2014. He is an icon in the hills and he is still driving the tractor; still representing this diverse group of growers who planted grapes and dreamed of starting a fledgling wine industry in the early decades of Oregon wine. Despite the appearance of international winegrowers, there are still many more potlucks than paparazzi in the vineyards along Worden Hill Road.

Allen Holstein was also honored with a star on the Ponzi Walk of Fame for his contribution to Oregon viticulture as a pioneering vineyard manager. In 1980 he purchased Gary Fuqua's Dundee Hills vineyard and built a house on the site. He is still farming the Knudsen Vineyard for Argyle Winery and growing grapes on his forty-two year old vineyard, which he has almost entirely replanted. Holstein, who was from Kentucky, came to Oregon in 1979 after a stint waiting tables in San Francisco with his college friend Ken Wright, where they discovered Oregon wines being served. After studying enology and viticulture at UC Davis, Ken came to Oregon in 1986 and formed Panther Creek Cellars with his former wife, Corby Stonebraker Soles.

Maresh and Holstein's recognition on the walk of fame is a significant acknowledgement for the remaining small group of pioneering grape growers. The original number of remaining growers has dwindled to a resilient group of Oregon wine pioneers who planted those first vines and hoped for the best. Their success is often overlooked by the media for larger commercial producers who own vineyards and produce their own wine. Their story is one of hard agricultural vineyard labor that began after they came home from their day jobs as engineers, doctors, business men and women. Their hard work paid off. They helped found an industry that has become a major economic contributor to the food, wine and travel industry of Oregon.

SECTION TWO: The Grower's Stories:

Abbey Ridge Vineyards/Cameron Winery
Bill and Julia Wayne/1977

Archibald Vineyard/Bill and Bessie Archibald/1971
current owners: Archery Summit Winery

Bauer Vineyards/Winderlea Winery
planted by John Bauer/1974
current owners: Bill Sweat and Donna Morris

Cleo's Hill Vineyard
current owners: Mike and Robin Murto

Holstein Vineyards/partially planted by Gary Fuqua/1972
current owner: Alan Holstein

Juliard Vineyards/Crumbled Rock Winery
partially planted by Tom Saucy/1972
current owners: Julia Staigers and Gerard Koschal

Knudscn-Erath Vineyards/Chateau St. Michelle
planted by Dick Erath, Kina Erath and Cal Knudsen/1969

Lange Vineyards/Lange Estate Winery
Don, Wendy and Jessie Lange/1984

Maresh Vineyards /Maresh-Arterberrry Winery/Powell Hill Winery
Loie and Jim Maresh Sr., Martha Maresh and Steve Mikami, Fred Arterberry, Jimmy Maresh/1970

McDaniel Vineyards and estate house/
Jim and Donna Jean McDaniel/1972
Torii Mor Winery/current owner: Don Olson

Weber Vineyards/Vivian and Arthur Weber/1973

Charles and Shirley Coury/Coury Vineyards 1965
currently Laurel Ridge Winery

The Grower's Stories

Jim and Donna Jean McDaniel:
McDaniel Vineyards
Torii Mor Winery

To my eight-year old ears, the word 'vine-yard' might as well have been from a foreign language. I didn't have the slightest idea what one was; and when I found out I was at best ambivalent, if not downright hostile, about the idea of leaving the McMinnville ranch house where I had lived my entire short life.

"Do I have to go?" I wailed.

When my parents announced their plans, I was aghast. Land was cheap then, although my father did sell his beloved sports car (a beautiful red Mercedes 290SL) to purchase three parcels of land in the Red Hills above Dundee, Oregon. It was 1973. The going price for land at the time was around fifteen-hundred dollars per acre.

Kerry and Jim McDaniel standing by vineyard plant stakes, McDaniel Vineyard, Dundee 1973.

Planting a vineyard and operating a winery certainly didn't hold the romantic connotations for me that it might have for many adults. It may have been easy for them to imagine the joys of languishing on a balcony, wineglass in hand, chatting casually about harvest. Although, as I was about to learn, no one ever chatted casually about harvest.

So what if a guy named David Lett had bought my family's old chicken processing plant in McMinnville and was making good wine - this meant nothing to me. Why did we have to try winemaking?

I went from the city to the country overnight. What I had considered an idyllic childhood - living in the city, following in my siblings footsteps at the local school - was suddenly shattered by my family's move to a trailer on fourteen acres of scrub field in rural Yamhill County. Bordered by plum and filbert orchards on the South side and oak trees on the North, this steeply sloping acreage was undeniably beautiful. I was non-plussed. I mean, not only was this not romantic for me, it wasn't even cool, which of course was everything in grade school circles.

"What's a vine-yard?" was the response from a new classmate of mine during the first week at my new alma mater - Dundee Grade School. I continued sulking.

My siblings on the other hand, two out of three who were attending college, were quick to recognize the potential benefits, summarized in two words: free wine.

This whole adventure started as a dream for my father, who longed to escape the stress of running the family grain elevator business. He wanted to grow grapes and make wine on an Oregon hillside for a number of reasons.

These reasons included following in the agricultural footsteps of his ancestors, who had been nurserymen in the Willamette Valley for generations, as well as a chance meeting with one of the founding fathers of the Oregon wine industry, David Lett of Eyrie vineyards. Lett came to Oregon to start a winery and bought a small chicken processing plant from McDaniel Grain and Feed. My Dad would wander down from the granary and watch Lett make wine. He was intrigued.

Planning the vineyard

By 1973 my parents owned three different pieces of potential vineyard property in the Red Hills. We began clearing and planting two, the fourteen-acre vineyard/house site, and the ten-acre site off nearby Worden Hill Road. They sold the third site the following year when they realized that three vineyards on three different locales were just too many to manage.

Note: today several wineries offer vineyard management crews for a select group of vineyards. In exchange for grapes, these wineries will manage a vineyard for the owner year round. Managing a vineyard includes maintenance and harvest of the grapes. This concept was unheard of in 1973. Family members, some willing, others only partially acquiescent, were the vineyard crew. In rare circumstances, when finances permitted, we hired a real crew for large tasks, such as planting or harvesting.

Our land was part of the original one hundred year-old Meyer farm. John Meyer sold us the land. At the time, his mother, the original owner of the farm, was still alive. Everyone called her Grandma Meyer. She lived in a small house on the farm, across from the bigger farmhouse. Originally, the road had ended at their farm, and the family enjoyed their seventy-five years of solitude while they lived on this peaceful dead end - and that's how they wanted to keep it.

John Meyer drove an old red farm truck when he wasn't on the tractor in the orchard, where he seemed to perpetually be, tilling or spraying. The hill sloped steeply down in a graceful arc and was still a productive prune and hazelnut orchard. Meyer maintained an immaculate farm, despite his advancing age. He was a kindhearted man who always waved from the tractor. Not an overzealous wave, just the one wave of the hand or touch of the hat so common to farmers and men of that generation.

This orchard became my playground. I would wander for hours discovering the natural springs that gushed out of the ground and formed little stream beds that foamed down the hillside, where a creek ran through the canyon. I also discovered an outhouse and an old prune dryer, both of which seemed terrifyingly macabre and decrepit. I never did go into the outhouse, but once I did enter the prune dryer, which turned out to be nothing more than a small shed. The floorboards creaked and I ran out of their as fast as I could. Mostly, I'd perch on the hillside, with the tremendous view beneath me, and read.

Grandma Meyer, who lived on the edge of the orchard, was a delightful Scottish woman who still had a brogue and made shortbread cookies. I remember her with great fondness, as I wandered over their often (she was the closest neighbor) during that first fall and started a friendship.

She often served me tea and shortbread, and like me, she was an avid reader. She always had the latest edition of Reader's Digest or National Geographic, which, while not my first choice, I enjoyed reading aloud to her anyway.

In the fall of 1974, we focused our energies on the Worden Hill Road Vineyard and on the house and winery site. I wore my favorite red wool plaid pants and held my father's hand as we walked the potential house site. At the time, the address was the old rural route designation, 'Route 1, Box 418', before the postal service changed in the late 1980s. Orange and yellow Maple leaves crunched under our feet as we walked the perimeter of the acreage. Dad talked about clearing the aged prune and walnut trees that dotted the hillside, and speculated about ways to control the ever-present blackberry bushes.

With a caterpillar tractor, on the weekends or after work at the mill, my father, brother Michael and anyone else who had been drafted started clearing the land. This tedious procedure took them many months but eventually rendered two beautifully cultivated fields of deep, red dirt.

While they were tilling, my father started the hunt for cedar end posts and stakes (cedar was still in bountiful supply in Oregon in the early 1970s). He bargained his way through lumberyards and eventually acquired enough wood to cut end posts and stakes for the vineyard.

He hauled them home on a flatbed truck and my parents began the tedious curing process. First, they poured weatherproofing Verathane in five-gallon buckets and stuck a stake in it. After a few hours, they turned the stakes and quickly realized they needed a faster way. With more than a little bit of ingenuity, Dad manufactured fifty-pound vats from old oil barrels, which he cut in half. Then they could cure more than one post at a time and sink the entire post in the liquid.

Each of these events took several telephone calls and much imagination.

"The next wave of growers built on our new found systems. We shared a lot of advice with Bill Wayne (Wayne vineyards, Cameron Winery), and in turn he shared with us. That was the way it was then. We all helped each other because no one really knew what they were doing anyway," my mother.

My father found the grape plants for the vineyard where just about everyone else did at the time - from Dick Erath and Charles Coury.

Grape cuttings look like six-inch sticks and are actually cuttings off the original mature grape vine. To plant them effectively, they need to flower naturally or on a nursery hotbed. Since Oregon rarely provides enough heat in early spring to flower these cuttings naturally dad drew on one of his nurserymen connections, his Uncle Kent McDaniel. Uncle Kent had been a successful rose propagator in Carlton, Oregon and had patented many famous varietals. His 'Cara Mia' deep red rose is still widely used in the floral industry today.

"It's a miracle we were able to plant 99% of each variety, because all they really look like is, well, a brown stick, until they flower," said dad.

Unbeknownst to us until a few years later, the Pinot noir section we planted wasn't purely Pinot noir. During a cool night, my brother returned from delivering the cuttings to the vineyard, where he kept them in small holding pots (holding nurseries were a common way to store the stock until we planted them). My brother thought the night was too cool to leave the truck with its cuttings outside on the Carlton Rose Nursery platform. So he opened a door into the warehouse and unloaded what was left of the cuttings, all in a pile on the warehouse floor. There was only one problem - they were not all Pinot noir cuttings; there were Gamay noir and Chardonnay cuttings on the truck too.

In a classic case of haste makes waste, when he and dad went back the next day, no one could tell what was what in the tremendous pile of brown sticks. They piled the cuttings back on the flatbed, hauled them to the house, and lined them up, four deep to a pile, in a semicircle around the driveway. We waited at least a week for them to flower, so we could take a vague guess at to what was what.

"You literally had to wade through the cuttings to get to the front door. We lived with that pile for at least a week. We got to laughing so hard one day about it, we named the pile 'Mike's Mix' and the name stuck", said Donna Jean.

We eventually sorted and planted 'Mike's Mix' in the Pinot noir section of the vineyard. For years to come, now and then a Gamay or Chardonnay vine would shoot straight up, in stark contrast to the Pinot vines that grew in a graceful arc. Even the Pinot noir wine that we eventually made from these grapes had distinct Gamay overtones.

Plotting

Our next obstacle was plotting and planting the vineyard. First, we laid out rows with a huge steel cable.

Getting a straight line wasn't easy, as my mother, the chief landscape architect on our staff recalled, "Jim brought the cable home and suggested that I could mark it every six feet. Every six feet, we put a blue tape on the cable. The cable was one inch thick. Every ten feet we put a yellow mark, which is where we put the stakes. The mathematics that it took to mark cable for fifty-foot rows was incredible. The steel cable was strung all over the house, and we just started measuring at one end."

Once the monumental task of marking the lightweight cables was completed, a feat, which Donna Jean recalled, took months but really only took about a week, they laid the cable out on the ground. At every blue mark, they dug a hole, and stuck in a grape cutting.

"Now they have very simple ways to plant a vineyard - a gigantic job for amateurs. But we didn't know what these simple ways were, so we made up our own rules," said Donna Jean.

Planting a vineyard separates true friends from occasional friends; some thought it would be fun to help. John Martin, a teenaged family friend labored day and night for extra college money. It was hard, dirty work - bending over all day, digging a six-inch hole and sticking a cutting in the hole, and then somehow securing a milk carton around the plant - then repeating the process about 3,000 times. All spring and summer we labored to plant both sites.

My job was to water the cuttings with a bucket of water drawn from the pump house. Each cutting, every day, all summer. Eventually we rigged a platform behind the tractor to haul water. One person could walk behind the tractor, and dip water out of a bucket on the back.

Each new problem required a creative solution.

"Marking, planting, watering, suffering...novices all," recalled mom.

Before long, cuttings lined the hillsides in long white lines at both vineyard sites. The vines were planted in holes about a foot deep and firmly ensconced in their milk carton jacket (the cartons deter the deer and other pests from eating the vines). On the sides of the cartons, local dairies with names like 'Alpenrose' and 'Mighty-Fine' advertised their wares to an expanse of field and the occasional hawk that flew by.

We planted hardy Pinot noir vines at the top of the vineyards. Below that, we planted a few acres of Chardonnay, followed by some Riesling, Muscat, Gamay noir and Sauvignon blanc.

By the middle of summer, we had completed the first planting. What plants the deer didn't eat or that didn't die from lack of water, actually survived and, to our surprise, flourished.

To follow, recalled mom, were much different tasks beyond our capacity, but when planting the vineyard, in the end 'good old-fashioned stubborn persistence paid off.'

There were a few other vineyards that had been planted on the surrounding hillsides in 1973 by local growers - Erath, Archibald, Weber, Maresh and Fuqua vineyards. Over the hill towards Dayton were the Sokol-Blosser and Lett families. The Ponzi's were establishing their vineyard and winery near Tigard and Charles

Coury had one near Forest Grove. Tualatin Vineyards, Oak Knoll and Elk Cove were also evolving. That was about it for the Willamette Valley. Richard Sommers was operating Hillcrest near Roseburg, and Southern Oregon vineyards were evolving rapidly too, although we had little contact with them.

First fall on the hill; building the house

My parents had not made this life changing decision lightly. They had four children, two in college, one a senior in a high school and the youngest (me); none of us had the urge to leave our well-established roots. In retrospect, my sister Claudia and I resisted the change most fervently, she didn't want to spend her senior year attending the rival high school and I didn't want to attend a different school, period.

My mother also had misgivings. She was a landscape architect and was perfectly happy ripping up other people's lawns and redesigning them. To her, building a home and planting a vineyard seemed like a tremendous undertaking that would require a great deal of energy.

But my parents came from a long line of ambitious, hardworking people who had the courage to follow their dreams. Besides, deep down, my mom relished the opportunity to design a new home.

One thing is for certain - neither of them had any idea when the Oregon wine industry would become the multimillion dollar industry that it is today.

So, there we were, our first fall on the hill, living in two travel trailers. My parents had sold the family house in McMinnville, planted a vineyard on half of their new land, and leveled the land for the new house, but the question still loomed in all of our minds, "What have we gotten ourselves into?"

I lived with my parents, two cairn terriers, a Lhasa apso and a lot of red dirt in my grandparent's former travel trailer. My older sister Claudia, the high school senior, resided gloomily alone in the other travel trailer, which my parents had borrowed from our generous family dentist.

It certainly was not a scene from "Falcon Crest."

To protect ourselves, our clothing and the interior of the trailers from the perpetual onslaught of heavy red mud we would spread newspaper out on the linoleum. Despite our best efforts, the soil seemed to get everywhere. It was impossible to remove.

I slept on the foldout couch in the eating nook that also doubled as the living room and kitchen. In the evenings, the four of us crammed onto the couch to eat dinner with the dogs begging expectantly below. Our intimate quarters had made us all cranky. Red mud from the muddy dogs caked the newspapers on the floor, which by dinnertime usually became a slippery wet mess. So this was vineyard living? At the time, many of these nights were more like a moody Moorish poem; replete with the rain pounding relentlessly on our metal home, the wind howling through the mossy oak trees, and the fog settling in like a gray blanket in the morning.

One evening, during the time my mother was preparing dinner, my father felt extreme heat emanating from the wall. The trailer wiring was overheating. We turned off the electricity and ate our half-cooked meal by the light of a propane lantern.

The project seemed to have taken on a life of its own.

Our driveway was a quarter mile of bumpy gravel road. We were three miles away from the closest town, Dundee, and at least a quarter mile away from our closest neighbors. To my father, the quiet solitude of life in the hills was an immediate escape from the stresses of running the mill in McMinnville. To my mother, this new lifestyle only strengthened her independent nature; she was undaunted by the drive to Dundee, McMinnville or Portland.

To me, it seemed like an imposed exile.

Those first few months we were connected to reality by a phone pole the phone company erected near the pump house (where we had recently drilled for a lot longer that we had wanted to for water). I still remember the sensation of standing outside, talking on the phone and leaning my back against the phone pole, gazing out at the spectacular panoramic vista as if I was in some kind of cosmic phone booth.

The whole valley lay at my feet in a perfect half bowl shape, with me standing on the rim. To the South, on a clear day, I could squint and see the shimmering glint from the gold man standing on top of the capitol in Salem. Straight ahead were the Cascade Mountains.

Building the house

The same carpenters who built my bus house also built me a split-level tree house on stilts amidst the oak trees outside the lower level of our house. This cleverly designed tree house looked like an architectural extension of our house. It embarrassed me.

"Why can't my tree house look like other people's tree houses? Why do I have to have a tree house with an Asian design influence?" I would wail to my father as he watered the bonsai and newly planted Japanese garden.

Evidently, my ideal home was a tract house, where 'normal' people live. And Lord knows, normalcy is everything to a grade-schooler. If I knew anything at the time, I knew that living on this vineyard was clearly not going to be 'normal.'

Left to right: Katie, Cairn Terrier; Jim McDaniel, Lauren and Warner Henderson pose by grape crates, McDaniel driveway, 1979.

These aesthetic tastes should not have been surprising, coming from the man who has spent the last forty years playing the piano every morning. For years, friends of mine would bolt straight up in bed when 5:30 a.m. strains of Chopin reverberated through the house.

"What the hell is that?" they would mumble with wild eyes.

My father's interest in Asian culture began in his youth. As an eighteen year-old in the Air Force, he was stationed as a hydroponics farmer in postwar occupied Japan. This experience eventually led to a degree in Asian Studies from the University of Oregon before he committed himself to a lifetime of work as a grain dealer in the family grain and seed business.

Over the years, his interest in Oriental culture stayed with him, and its influence can be seen in the architecture of both of my two childhood homes. Cedar fences of varying heights and a Japanese garden surrounded both houses. Anchoring the Japanese shrine affect was a huge, traditional Japanese gate over the driveways.

I knew what feng shui was before I knew how to ride a bike. In retrospect, both of my parent's far-ranging interests have had a profound influence on my life. At the time, I desperately wanted a 'normal house' and snack pack pudding. Instead, I learned to eat with chopsticks and tell the difference in red wines by smell and sight, and, with a puckered face, taste (long before I ever drank them for pleasure).

We had custom-built Bonsai tables where most people would have a patio set. While other children picked strawberries, I watered Bonsai and pruned grapevines.

Our vineyard house was more like a Japanese roadhouse than an American colonial. Besides the pocket doors and cedar-lined walls, we had tatami mats in the entry and oriental teakwood benches in the living room. There was a Japanese soaking tub in the downstairs bathroom, which was useless unless you had an abundant water supply, which we did not. (Years later, high school friends dubbed the house "pachinko palace" and languished in the soaking tub, drinking glasses of too young Pinot. Alas, those days were still on the horizon).

But even a house with feng shui, (including a red front door and a basket of slippers to put on when entering) would have been preferable to the travel trailers we inhabited all that fall.

The foundation site had to be level and deep to allow for the ten-foot high cement foundation, which would eventually house the winery. This proved to be very expensive, and became one of many items that came in over budget on a project that quickly ballooned in cost. All told, when the house was completed, it cost one-hundred and fifty-thousand dollars although my parents initial budgeting suggested that seventy-five thousand dollars should have been enough.

The cedar siding and shakes for the roof arrived from the mill in Canada so wet that they could have practically floated down themselves. They were promptly sent back in disgust. The second batch of siding and shingles, my parents decided, needed to be cured to preserve them, and so we built huge cattle troughs for the job. Day and night we soaked, turned, dipped and stacked siding and shingles.

Things never seemed to go smoothly. We wanted all the utility wires to be underground, for obvious aesthetic reasons. Then, when we were grading the ground and tilling for the lawn, we inadvertently chopped up the carefully laid utility wires. This necessitated, once again, answering the phone in the pump house/cosmic phone booth.

My parent's goal with the house had been to make it fit into the hillside as 'organically as the prune dryers of the past century, molding naturally into the hillside.'

We continued to sleep in the travel trailers and stored our personal belongings in the newly poured foundation of the winery, piled up in 6-foot high clothing storage boxes, which lined the walls. We lived in this manner for another six months.

Dad begged the builder to allow our life to return to some sort of normalcy and convinced them to finish the kitchen, while miles of molding remained to be mounted.

Moving day finally came, and we moved into the red-floored kitchen, ingeniously color coordinated to match the red mud outside, which we had learned had a way of coming inside, whether you wanted it to or not.

As the men bought the white refrigerator in, my mother said, "It just isn't right. Take it back out and put it in my pickup."

My dad sighed, shook his head, and then let her take the fridge to an auto body shop, where she had it painted fire engine red.

We moved in the day before Christmas. We had little time to decorate. My parents told us we could put up anything we wanted. We gleefully went out and chopped down a fir tree that was thirty feet tall from our nearby woods. My brother forced it through the double front door and threw decorations at it from the balcony loft. My mother left the room in horror, which was a tactical error. My brother promptly picked up a hammer and six very large nails and pounded six very large holes above our newly finished mantel for our Christmas stockings. The wall later required refinishing.

Carried away by enthusiasm, we stuffed the large fireplace with slightly soggy, mossy wood and construction leftovers, and lit a fire, which promptly filled the room with smoke until it billowed out the doors.

Thus began our first merry vineyard Christmas.

Dundee

When we moved to Dundee, which is located along highway 99W between Newberg, Oregon and McMinnville, Oregon it was a bucolic backwater town. Dundee store was the cultural hub in this small community of 500 people. Beer and candy bars were its main staple.

Besides Dundee store, the Nighthawk cafe ran a close second for local culture, where truckers went for their donuts and coffee. The Nighthawk is now Tina's, an upscale restaurant. But, since the 1950s the Nighthawk cafe functioned and looked just like countless little truck stops throughout in the United States. There was the classic neon sign on a pole, in the shape of an arrow that read "Nighthawk Cafe". The cafe itself was a small, cement box. Inside was a bar in a semicircle with attached bar stools that spun. You could smell and see the fry cook in the kitchen. The waitress always seemed to be pouring coffee into the bottomless cup of a perpetual trucker.

At that time, it seemed like Dundee had one policeman, who spent most of his time upholding the town's well earned reputation as a 'speed trap'. Although today there often seems to be a perpetual traffic jam in Dundee, in the early 1970s you really could speed through town. These 'speeders' gave Dundee's policeman a reason for being, and he lurked near the highway for most of his shift, occasionally switching places to get a better vantage point from which to nab his next victim. The rest of his shift was spent patronizing the Nighthawk.

Besides Dundee store and the Nighthawk, the main drag through town featured a drive-in burger joint and the Dundee Women's Hall, which always confused me - what about the Dundee men's hall?

If you continued driving north through town on 99W, you encountered the Hickory House Tavern (now Lumpy's), a '76 gas station, the post office, fire hall, city hall, a shop called Nut World (no joke), the Hobby Hut, the Horsetrader (a rock hound shop) and finally, the elementary school. There was not a stoplight. The student crossing guards bravely took their life into their hands each morning and afternoon and shuttled children across the road.

Although many of these business are now gone, at the time they were bona fide, local attractions that helped define the eccentric atmosphere in this small town.

The Horsetrader was a strange conglomeration of products housed in a warehouse next to the Nut World. Basically, it was a surplus hardware store, the owner, by his own admission, a genuine horsetrader. You could find a variety of nails and Legg's pantyhose plastic eggs in the same bucket, both for sale at discount prices.

The Hobby Hut was a popular craft house for the under 12 and over 60 year-old crowd. For me the biggest draw was the toll painting and town gossip. I have no idea how many lawn elves, useless cement plaques and small cement animals I produced in this wonderful little shop.

Nut World, in particular, fascinated me. Nut World was located in a large brown building facing the highway with 'Nut World' in large, white wooden letters and a giant squirrel embellishing the facade. The giant squirrel attracted almost as much attention as the name itself. Inside was a small retail store with a nut and fruit drying facility. Twenty-five years later, the huge cement warehouse that housed the drying facility would become Argyle Winery. But in the early 70's, the days of wineries lining the streets of Dundee were still far away.

Occasionally I would wander around the aisles at Nut World after school, eating samples and learning the names of the nuts and fruits that lined the room in large, bulk bins. Dundee was at the time, and may still be, the self proclaimed 'hazelnut capital of the world'. Obviously, this was the town's main staple, as were dried walnuts, prunes and other fruits – but that is someone else's story.

The county was a logical place for agricultural business to flourish. I learned to enjoy the seasons while driving through the countryside on 99W from McMinnville to Dundee. There were several fruit stands featuring local produce along the road. During that first fall, we routinely stopped at one or more of these stands and bought squash, cucumbers, potatoes and other seasonal produce. In the spring, we filled our freezer with strawberries and raspberries, and later in the season, fresh corn, peaches and blackberries.

I spent hours exploring the countryside on foot. I walked to our neighbors - the Mareshes, Webers and Fuquas, and to the Dundee store, trying to develop the shortest possible routes to each destination without using the main road. My hikes down, up and over the hilltops resembled the up and down of a roller coaster. Out the driveway and down the washboard road to the bottom of the hill I veered to the right, straight up through an old prune orchard and overgrown tractor road, (there being many of both of these at the time). I waded slowly up this particular abandoned road, through the waist high grass and underbrush until I emerged into the clearing of our first vineyard at the top of the hill - which is now bordered by the new Erath winery. There, at the top of the hill, the orchards, occasional vineyard and fir trees lay together like pieces of a patchwork quilt.

One of my first hikes, and eventually my favorite, was a walk on an old wagon trail road, which was located on the bottom of a ravine between our hill and the neighboring Fuqua vineyard to see my friend Paige. I would plunge through the woods that lined the bottom of the vineyard and walk straight down through the woods for at least half a mile. This downhill plunge took me through a forest of tall fir trees, underbrush, and clearings strewn with cones and needles. I learned that deer slept in these clearings and I tried to be as quiet as I could, hoping to catch a glimpse of them. At the bottom of the ravine was the wagon road.

The wagon road itself began at what is now the Dundee watershed. It snaked its way through our valley in the Red Hills, following a creek, and ended in the Chehalem Valley. There is much speculation about it's origin's - some say it was a road used by Ewing Young as he transversed the valley to his homestead, located on what is now Hwy 240. It was obviously in use by the turn of the century. It still had ruts in the dirt when I was walking on it.

The vineyard matures and so do I - Girl Scout tying crew

I grew up along with the vineyard. The vineyard turned five and I turned thirteen. It was finally time for our first real harvest. I wore braces and bellbottoms, (San Francisco Riding Gear). To complete the ensemble, I donned a terrycloth tennis visor and a tube top as I tied grapes in the spring of 1979.

To this day, certain songs instantly bring back that time in my life; 'Sailing' by Christopher Cross, 'Baker Street' by Gerry Rafferty, and almost any disco. I had a little black transistor radio that leeched the life out of four huge batteries almost every day. I played it as loud as I could, not as if anyone could hear it.

Desperate for summer labor, my father once hired my entire Girl Scout troop to tie vines. To the Girl Scouts, this job looked immensely more appealing than the alternative: picking strawberries, so he got a good turnout.

Ten adolescent girls joined me in the vineyard, and you can about guess the rest. When we weren't applying suntan lotion that smelled like ripe coconuts, we were lounging between the rows trying to get a good tan, the bravest of us stripped down to our underwear. We stationed a sentinel - when we spotted my Dad we leapt back up and commenced tying.

Harvest recollections

Harvesting grapes is not an intellectual event; it's a carefully orchestrated physical marathon.

"Boom", a muffled shot would ricochet through the hills. It was met about a minute later with a retort that sounded like fireworks being shot into the air.

Harvest time - and all over the surrounding hillsides bird cannons were going off in no consecutive order. The cannons, which were actually small metal noisemakers, would erupt in their never-ending battle against hungry birds. You didn't want to be too close when they went off or your eardrums rang from the force of the shot.

I would set the cannon for timed eruption and run as fast as I could, waiting for the explosion.

'Kaboom' - it came before I was halfway down the row. Caught again. Still, at least I knew the cannon was operating and my job was done.

Like all grape growers, then and now, we tried various ways to rid the vineyard of birds. Deer were never as much of a problem - they feared confinement and refused to walk down a row; claustrophobia made them more of a pest at the end of the rows, were they would investigate three or four plants for ripe fruit.

The birds, however, were different. The story of how birds would jump three feet into the air when the cannon went of and then settle back down on top of the grapes again became urban legend. Despite our best efforts, the birds were only briefly distracted from the feast of ripe grapes.

We used various techniques to rid ourselves of the determined flocks, most of them nonviolent. One year when the birds were particularly bad, my grandfather took a rifle and with his crack shot eliminated some of the more persistent starlings and robins, which were the most common pests. I was not pleased with this approach.

There were two or three kinds of bird shots. My brother shot flares into the air with a streamer gun. Flares with a tail of smoke blazed over the vines and reeked of gunpowder. These flares also let out a high-pitched wine, which in theory was also supposed to deter the birds.

My mother was quickly taken off the bird patrol after she shot the gun backwards. The flare narrowly missed her as it wailed down the driveway. She demoted herself to the bird-free sanctuary inside the house.

Another method to protect the ripening crop was to roll net out over the entire row. This tremendously time consuming, expensive procedure involved literally rolling a huge net off a spool, which we then dragged like a shroud over all the rows from beginning to end. After about five feet, the net would inevitably get tangled like Saran Wrap in the vines. We would diligently untangle the whole mess and start over. The more dedicated birds always found a way in anyway.

Probably the most inane bird deterrent was the 'hawk kite '. These were not artistic masterpieces, and it showed. The hawk is a very hard design to reproduce in kite form. It didn't take long for the robins and star-lings to figure out that these helium filled balloons, strung ten feet up in the air suspended from the stakes, were not their mortal enemies. Mostly they made the vineyard look like a giant carnival tent.

Waiting for the grapes to ripen and reach ideal sugar content, or 'brix' is an art, not a science, just like harvesting many other agricultural products. The key to timing the harvest correctly depends on guessing the weather for the next month and relying on your gut instinct. You do not want to pick them too early or they will not have enough sugar or taste in the fruit to make a decent wine. However, you do not want to pick them too late, and risk harvesting rotten fruit. You also pray for sunshine, because if you leave them on the vine and a heavy rain comes, it could decimate the fruit. On the flip side, too much sunshine can dry out your fruit; too little can hamper its ability to ripen. All these factors usually make the weeks before harvest a tense waiting game.

However, when the time is right - or when your patience runs out and you guess this is as good a time as any - the harvest begins. While time before harvest seems to standstill - when harvest actually starts time accelerates.

Up at sunup, the harvest crew is picking as fast as they can, for as long as they can, until they fall into bed and repeat the process the next day. In the beginning, the crew was us; my parents, brother, grandparents and whatever hapless family friend was lured into the cause. While we all remember this fondly in hindsight, the reality was both exciting and exhausting.

In Oregon, the delicate process of ripening a grape depends primarily on when the rain will come. Some years, when we'd measured just enough brix on the refractometer and the barometer was dropping, we'd rush out and try to beat the rain. Rarely were harvests picture perfect; most seemed to be more like a frantic rush to save the endangered fruit on the vine from inclement weather and pests.

Most vineyards don't produce any grapes of consequence for at least four years - six years is ideal. We harvested grapes from the fourth year on, mostly because we really were just growing grapes to make our own wine. Eventually, when the vineyard reached maturity, it started producing more tonnage, which we sold to the few locally operating wineries, Knudsen-Erath, Coury and Adelsheim. These people were both growing grapes and making wine. We, on the other hand, were just growers on a different part of the wine food chain.

Making the wine

In the early years of the industry, there was little distinction between the growers and the winemakers. Most of us both grew grapes and made wine - either in our basements or in crudely constructed wineries. Frequently these wineries were old barns, laundry rooms or wherever else we could marginally insulate. Dick Erath had carboys and barrels scattered around his house and front porch. David Lett lived in a trailer on his newly planted vineyard and made wine in an old processing plant. Gary Fuqua had his wine barrels and his washing machine in the same room. Even Richard Sommers of Hillcrest in Roseburg, the modern winemaking era's first true winemaker, did everything himself; planting, harvesting, pressing and making the wine.

This group, however, had lofty goals. They had vision and foresight. Mostly, they were willing to work hard and make the needed sacrifice to realize their dreams. Although this was still the 'Mom and Pop' era, my dad always said that once the big corporations appeared, the industry would take off.

Everyone had a 'regular job' during the day. The dream was costly. Many growers planted and maintained their vineyards on vacation days, with family help. The charm of the early years of the Oregon wine industry centered on these simple beginnings. Some of the wines produced in these makeshift wineries were stupendous, and some were not.

Like other grower's, we crushed grapes for personal vintages in our basement. We had to innovate. If we didn't have a stemmer crusher, we borrowed one. We recycled wine bottles, washed them in the bathtub, and used them for the next year's crush. We handmade our labels or wrote in gold pen on the bottles. Sometimes we just marked the top of the corks with different colored pens 'PN78' or 'CH78' (pinot noir 1978, chardonnay, etc).

There were no vineyard supply stores. If you wanted a tractor to plow your land, you went to John Deere tractor or a farm equipment store. If you wanted winemaking supplies, you went to Steinbart's, a beer distributor in Southeast Portland, where you could modify various beer making apparatus. Mostly we used a lot of plastic tubing, carboys and sulfur pellets, and depended on the local farming and agricultural supply stores.

Dad bought a Lamborghini tractor, which my brother promptly dubbed, the 'sports tractor'. It was a crawler tractor, designed to crawl up steep Italian vineyard hillsides. It malfunctioned from the start, going in complete circles when you put it in gear or not moving at all. When it did work, it was so heavy it was hard to control. Once, vainly trying to put the brakes on, dad coasted downhill past the vineyard and ended twenty feet later in the woods, scraped up but still in the seat.

Much to our amazement, after a few years the vines began producing grapes. I loved eating the fruit straight from the vine. Our dogs gorged themselves on them. Every harvest we made grape juice, and filled the freezer full of Tupperware containers.

When the grapes were fermenting in tanks, the fruit flies covered the bathroom mirror. We would get up and the mirrors would be black with flies.

During one of our harvests, my grandfather backed up a short bed truck, loaded with bins, and slammed on the brakes. Fruit cascaded in waves all over the driveway. My mother said she could have thrown chili all over everything she was so frustrated with the whole process.

One time, a three-piece jazz combo played on the porch while we crushed grapes on the cement pad below. This particular harvest was picture perfect - bright sunny skies and crisp, cool weather. We had to yell to hear the chorus of 'Mack the Knife', but no one cared, we were a jovial crew. My parents had enlisted unsuspecting and willing friends and family who came looking more for a good time than a good job, which pretty much summed up the wine industry in the early eighties: more of a good time than a good job.

Significant people in my life emerged from this group. Betsy and Gary Johnson and their family were fresh off the boat from Hawaii. Rollin Soles was in our basement helping my father direct the crew. He was creating one of his first Oregon vintages – and our last. He went on the establish one of Oregon's premier sparkling wine houses.

We organized a sort of an assembly line, team approach to the whole crushing process. What it lacked in finesse, it made up for in style. We fortified the participants with Pinot noir, music, and a smorgasbord of food.

Since the cement pad outside the basement was large enough to accommodate the stemmer-crusher, the more stalwart members of the crew - those strong enough to hoist wooden crates of cut grapes up to shoulder level - diligently fed the crusher with boxes of grapes. Grape juice spilled out one end of the machine.

This time was an era of great experimentation for many winemakers. At a neighboring winery during this particular crush, an assistant winemaker stripped off his clothes and jumped naked into a stainless steel vat to warm up newly picked grapes. When the winemaker found him, he was submerged up to his neck in the juice. He was fired post haste, but achieved everlasting fame for his performance.

Bottling

Bottling was a rigorous process involving many steps. In our quest to master the fine art of winemaking, we undertook and even managed to complete most of these steps, despite the various mishaps along the way.

I was the corking girl. Anyone who has ever hand corked wine bottles (or beer bottles for that matter) will understand how important proper technique is in this position. If you fill the bottles too full, the cork displaces the wine - basically, the wine sprays like a shaken up champagne bottle, up into your face.

The muscles in my left arm ached, and the smell of sulfur burned in my nostrils, but I kept the rhythm; drop cork, pull handle, remove bottle, put bottle in case. I felt martyred, this bottling girl/cellar rat didn't always agree with the

Rollin Soles and Jim McDaniel making wine in basement McDaniel Vineyards 1985

grain dealer/winemaker, but I continued to work in the basement anyway. Our work time together evolved into my first paying job, and I loved my father despite the turbulent pains of growing up and learning responsibility.

Before we were able to cork the bottles, we had to get the wine in them. Bottling in the early years was a primitive process usually involving yards of lab tubing, garden hoses, recycled wine bottles or wine bottles bought from Steinbarts. We also set up two stainless steel sinks filled with hot soapy water, where we soaked recycled bottles until their labels came off.

On bottling days, the cement floor of the basement was a slippery mess of grape pressings and water. The air was a steam bath filled with the scent of fermenting grapes and sulfur. We sloshed around in our knee high rubber boots and tried not to break our necks sliding on the slippery cement, or be electrocuted from the various power cords strung about the floor. What we lacked in glamour we made up for in raw enthusiasm.

Since we were also lacking in professional training, we relied solely on experimental techniques. We bottled two different ways. The first, more basic method was the carboy/barrel siphoning technique; and the second, once we acquired more equipment, was the standard bottling machine technique.

The carboy/barrel technique was straightforward, and involved a lot of spitting for the bottler to continue soberly. Using laboratory tubing, Dad would insert one end of the tube into the carboy, and the other end into his mouth. Then he would squat down and suck as hard as he could, which brought the wine flowing through the tube. Then he would hand me the tube, whose flow we controlled by kinking it in the middle like a garden hose, and I would begin my frantic filling of the bottles, one by one.

Remembering that this process is all gravity dependent, I had to keep the hose down lower than the top of the carboy, which is only about two and a half feet high. I am convinced that using this process is where the 'happy winemaker' stereotype comes from. Often the flow would stop; I could only bend down so long to fill each bottle. Inevitably, dad would have to restart the tube, and sometimes he'd be in such a hurry he'd forget to spit. Well, while he certainly wasn't drunk by the end of the day's bottling, his cheeks used to get quite rosy.

After our first year of production, we moved onto the second, more sophisticated bottling technique, although even this was fraught with its own perils. By this time, we had acquired some barrels and a few tanks to store the wine in, together with the aforementioned carboys. This uptake in production meant we had to refine our process for getting the wine into the bottle.

We still used a lot of lab tubing, but this time we strung the tubes across the floor, from the barrels, and into the small bottling machine powered by an electric pump. When our bottling line was in full swing, we had several quarts of wine per minute flowing through the bottling machine, which had smaller pumps hanging from it that resembled udders. We hooked six wine bottles at a time to the udders, and filled each one simultaneously, at slightly different rates. This meant the law of gravity, again, controlled the situation more than we did. Invariably, a bottle would fill up before I could grab it, and shoot wine straight out the top in a showering arc. I would grab these bottles as fast as I could, but the whole process often resembled the frantic conveyer belt scene from 'I Love Lucy'. When more than one bottle was spewing, we would shut the pump down and go back to our other flow speed - unbearably slow. Somehow, we still managed to bottle many cases of wine at a time.

We filled the bottles then placed them on tables, where they sat until we corked them. Since bottling sometimes took several days, we didn't always cork them immediately when they came off the line.

We did learn, however, that storing wine and on tables uncorked wasn't the smartest idea in the world. Once, in a matter of seconds, disaster struck as dad walked over to check on at least 250 bottles of wine standing on top of four slightly rickety foldout picnic tables. Whether it was the vibration of his footsteps, or a combination of rickety tables and vibration, we'll never know, but one of the picnic tables collapsed, which sent wine bottles like bowling pins into each other before they crashed to the floor. These falling bottles created an avalanche into the remaining three tables of wine bottles. Time stood still, seconds that seemed like minutes ticked by as dad and I watched and listened in horrible disbelief at the cacophony of wine bottles exploding on the floor. Shards of glass floated in the inch deep lake of Pinot noir.

Neither of us knew whether to cry of laugh. We just stood their without uttering a sound, although out of the corner of my eye I saw dad struggling to control his temper. As the waves of Pinot swirled around his boots, dad looked down and stamped his feet in frustration, uttering a resounding curse as he splashed red wine all over himself and me. Of course, the sight of both of us, covered in red wine, immediately collapsed us into a fit of laughter.

Estimating that he had lost at least one thousand dollars worth of wine in that episode, we ended our bottling activity for the day.

Vineyard Parties

Yes, there were parties. It is probably the one thing that people are most curious about when they find out I grew up on a vineyard. When I moved there I was eight and didn't drink. I waited until I was sixteen and then mixed 1980 Pinot noir with Tang, which made my father cry, and not because he had caught me drinking, either....

We had many potluck parties at each other's houses back then. This seemed to be the preferable way to socialize. Most people went to work during the day, and then came home to work in the vineyard at night. No one ever got enough sleep. It was obvious they all felt passionate about what they were doing, because it took extraordinary effort just to make land payments and grow decent grapes.

There were always parties at harvest

Knudsen-Erath winery celebrated one of their first crushes by throwing a large harvest party. Cal Knudsen was vice-president of Weyerhaeuser in Seattle at the time and he had many affluent friends. He felt that introducing Oregon wine to this posh group would be good publicity for all the growers and winemakers in the area.

1985 Pinot noir label, McDaniel Winery

Knudsen decided to give away their first pressing. They invited an affluent crowd. One woman emerged from a Jaguar wearing a Pendleton skirt and a cashmere sweater holding a dainty pair of gardening shears, ready to pick grapes. Expensive cars filled the gravel parking lot and overflowed into the muddy vineyard.

These immaculately attired guests, dressed more for a country club lunch than a day picking grapes, swept grandly into the vineyard. What ensued was comic chaos. Most only made it about six feet down a row before they realized they were walking in mud. At this point, they became slightly flustered and unsure of how to continue. They would gamely bend down, and then flail with their pathetically inappropriate gardening shears, most of which were about as sharp as butter knives. After much sawing and mutilating of vines, eventually the cluster of grapes would drop into the bucket. Most of the guests petered out after picking just one bucket of grapes, and began to look for sustenance.

To help serve this crowd, Julia Lee Knudsen recruited all the neighbors, who ranged in daytime occupations from engineers to grain dealers, as a workforce that, in her words, turned out to be 'really not too manageable.'

My mother recalled, "While the party was supposed to be a place where the elite meet to eat, it was really about who thought they were the most elite - the guests or the servers."

Julia displayed her Russian Samovar antique urns and silver-plated coffee pots prominently on tables.

She declared that an antique press and gorgeous carvings, "Will help link us to great wine regions of the world."

The rebellious servers were to manage soup distribution and wander among the crowd filling wine glasses. The servers rebelled and started immediately drinking in the corner.

When one woman, clad from head to toe in a Channel suit asked a server for a bowl of soup, he snapped, "Get it yourself."

Later in the meal, Grandpa Erath, a cooper from Germany, was encouraged to sing. He had a beautiful booming voice and fit the role perfectly. It was opera in the vineyard.

"An elite group of drinkers served by a less than humble group of winemakers," described my mother.

Arthur and Vivian Weber:
Weber Vineyards

The couple bought twenty-one acres in 1972 in the Red Hills. They later bought a farmhouse and sixty-five adjacent acres in 1976. Between 1975 and 1988, they planted thirty-five acres of Pinot noir, Chardonnay and Riesling grapes.

Arthur Weber knew that the Red Hills of Dundee would be a great wine growing region when he tasted some of Dick Erath's first Pinot noir. There was no doubt in his mind that eventually these wines would mature, along with their winemakers, and gain international notoriety. Weber had foresight and drive and he knew he wanted to participate.

His wife, Vivian, had her own opinion - namely when they were going back

Arthur Weber, standing in Weber Vineyard, Dundee Hills, 1975.

to their hometown of Boston and when would it stop raining?

Arthur, who worked in the publishing industry, first ran into David Lett at the Oregon State University Math Department in the mid 1960s. Lett, like Arthur, was a book salesman.

Arthur said, "So what are you up to these days?"

Lett said, "Well, I'm selling books now but I'm really planning on being a winemaker."

Lett's subject intrigued Arthur. They conversed in detail about the fledgling Oregon wine industry. Arthur had been exploring California's wine industry, hoping to buy vineyard land in the already prosperous region. At the time, Oregon's land seemed more affordable than California's five thousand dollars an acre. Weber returned to Boston with a plan hatching in his fertile mind.

He convinced Vivian that instead of vacationing in Europe, as they had originally planned, they should vacation in Oregon instead. Vivian eventually relented and in the spring of 1971, the Weber's vacationed in Oregon.

"I didn't exactly feel like we were on the forefront of establishing an industry. I was really more interested in a cultural experience; and I was particularly interested in if the gray, rainy weather would ever abate," remembers Vivian.

The Webers decided that finding David Lett and talking to him about the fledgling industry was a good way to assess the situation. The problem was, Vivian recalled, that they really didn't know exactly what road to take once they arrived in Dundee. Of course Lett wasn't even in Dundee, he lived a few miles south down highway 99W, but this was beside the point.

So, in search of the elusive Lett, the Weber's innocently inquired at the lone gas station in Dundee as to where they might find the man who eventually became known as "Papa Pinot". Although they never did find "Papa Pinot" on this particular trip, they did make a discovery that began a lifelong friendship.

"Do you know where I might find a David Lett?" Arthur asked the gas station attendant.

The attendant casually gestured up the road, which happened to be Ninth Street in Dundee, and said, "I think he might live in that direction."

In this moment of serendipity, the Weber's innocently discovered their vineyard acreage, and their home to be.

So, they drove up Ninth Street, in search of the elusive Lett. At first, they passed through a small neighborhood of rundown houses that held little promise. They continued up the road, and as the elevation continued to climb, they saw hazelnut orchards. The rolling hills were getting steeper. A few farmhouses and driveways appeared. At the end of one, Weber saw a sign that read, 'Land for sale. Possible vineyard acreage.'

Arthur stopped the car at the end of the driveway. They glanced around. Down the driveway was a neat, green and white farmhouse, surrounded by filbert, plum and cherry orchards. On the other side of the road were a red barn, and a neat rows of grapes planted in the rich red soil. Beyond that, a spectacular panorama of the Willamette Valley appeared.

"Maybe this is Lett's house?" Arthur said.

They drove slowly down the driveway and parked the car in front of the house. Simultaneously, a huge, hairy German Shepard bounded up to the door and window of the car, barking furiously at Vivian as Arthur noticed another sign that said "please stay in car and honk for attention' or something to that affect.

"This adventure was taking a risky turn", thought Vivian.

The German Shepard, Herman the German, continued to assault the car for what seemed like hours until finally a man appeared. He called Herman off the car, and said hello. His wife came out on the front porch.

Weber, beside himself with enthusiasm, bounded out of the car and started talking to the man he thought was Lett about the vineyard land for sale, and planting vineyards, and anything else related to growing grapes; this although this man really didn't look much like the Lett he remembered.

Suddenly the man turned to Weber and said, "Look, I think you think I'm David Lett because you keep calling me David. My name is Jim Maresh, but I do have some vineyard land for sale."

As a result of this chance meeting, the Weber's purchased their first vineyard acreage, perched high on top of the Dundee Hills with a panoramic view of the Willamette Valley to the Cascade Mountains.

Arthur described the next few years of their life as 'very busy.' They flew back and forth between Boston and Dundee. Vivian, who was fluent in Spanish, continued working as a travel manager. Arthur had quit his job in publishing, although he would go back to the publishing business later. When they were in Dundee, they lived in a cabin above the fledgling Knudsen Erath vineyard and winery. Slowly, a community of growers and winemakers was forming.

Intermittent cabin living became a bit tedious for the Weber's. Even though they were planting a vineyard on their land, there was no advantageous place to build a house, and they had stretched themselves financially by buying the land first.

But, it was a magic time and place in the Red Hills, with a little help from Loie Maresh. Loie and Jim had become good friends and confidantes of the Webers in the short time the two families had been acquainted.

One day Loie quietly remarked to Arthur, in her remarkable, insightful way, "Buy Vivian a house, Arthur. That's really the way to make her happy. She doesn't want to live in a plane or a cabin for the rest of her life."

Shortly thereafter, the Weber's bought a farmhouse and existing acreage from Nita Moyer which, conveniently, bordered their existing vineyard site.

Planting the vineyard

The Weber's sited their vineyard on a prime slope above their house. They planted the first vines, Riesling, in 1975 with help from family and friends. Between 1975 and 1988, they planted a total of thirty-five acres of Pinot noir, Chardonnay, Riesling and some Gewurtraminer. Over the years, the Weber's have sold their grapes to Dick Erath, Arterberry Winery, Oak Knoll, Cameron and Rex Hill.

"No one really knew what type of grape was going to work," recalled Vivian.

Eddie Weber driving the tractor. Elly Miles and Vivian water plant starts in milk cartons in Weber Vineyards, 1976.

Jim and Loie Maresh:
Maresh Vineyards, Retreat Center and
Red Barn Tasting Room

Jim and Loie Maresh bought their Oregon farm in 1959. They were among the first Oregon farmers in the modern wine era to grow commercial wine grapes. The family still owns the farm, vineyards, retreat center and Maresh Red Barn. What started as a small farming venture is now a world-class Oregon vineyard, producing grapes for Arterberry-Maresh, Powell Hill and other local wineries.

The following is from an interview with Jim Maresh:

"Why should not some Oregon Valley, tilted at a certain angle to the sun, prove capable of producing wines as great as Europe's, but different from them, as Bordeaux is from Burgundy and Chablis is from Mosel, some new kind of supremacy of bouquet that will permanently enrich mankind," wrote Martha Maresh in 1971, at one of the first official Oregon winemaker meetings, held in the Maresh living room. She taped the paper banner, a loosely defined mission statement, to the fireplace.

A handful of vineyard growers had gathered that evening to discuss growing grapes in Oregon with Yamhill County extension agent Wayne Davis.

Jim and Loie Maresh pose in the Red Barn tasting room

Present that evening were Jim Maresh, Dick Erath, Bill Blosser, David Lett, Gary Fuqua, and Ron Vulsteke.

"I wish I would have taken a picture of all of us, we all had hair then," said Jim.

Long before that fortuitous early winemaker's meeting, Jim and Loie Maresh met in 1946 as students at Marquette University in Wisconsin. Jim was in the Naval Reserves. Loie was studying education and eventually would teach reading specialization. Neither of them had the slightest idea that one day they would be growing wine grapes in the epicenter of the emerging Oregon wine industry.

Loie and Jim were married in the late 1940 s and honeymooned at Timberline Lodge.

Several years later Jim was working for Dunn and Bradstreet in San Francisco when the company transferred him back to Oregon. The Maresh's were fond of Oregon; they had owned a home in Laurelhurst in the mid-50s. They immediately began searching for a view lot in the country.

However, things were a little different in the Red Hills from the hills of San Francisco. In San Francisco, Jim commuted from Los Altos to his office in one hour. From Dundee, he could drive from his farm to downtown Portland in 32 minutes. There was no stoplight in Newberg in 1959. There were also no bars or liquor stores until the early 1980s. They bought wine at Bargain City, just beyond the Newberg City limits. There was one traffic light on Hall Boulevard. There was nothing along Highway 99W at Sherwood; it was known simply as "Six Corners".

Jim recalled the day they found the farm:

"Loie and I went up there with Mary Grace, who was just a baby. We just wanted to buy a few acres; instead, we bought many acres of prunes, cherries, filberts, because the widow who owned it wanted to sell the whole thing.

I got home the first day of work and asked Loie how it went, and she went 'Oh God'. She had five kids on her hands, who were used to sidewalks, where they could roller-skate and play with neighbor kids. And then she said, 'I sure hope we can sell this dog of a farm for what we paid for it.' I will never forget that remark."

Jim continues: "Then after a while, we got the kid's horses and chickens, did the whole farm bit, and we really began to fall in love with the place. This was spring of 1959. Ten years later, just before Dick Erath came, there were many farmers who wanted to retire, so we bought acreage on top of the hill beside the house, and we bought the Herring place across the road. We let Joe Herring live in the house - the kids loved him.

We bought another old prune orchard, which became Arthur Weber's first piece of property. We sold it to him for fifteen-hundred an acre.

When Arthur sold it years later, I asked him,

"Did you mark it up a little bit from what you paid for it?"

He said, "Yea, I added a number of zeros."

Winemakers and Farmers

Maresh eventually had three simultaneous careers. He worked for a Fortune 500 company, was a full-time farmer, and had a military career as a commander in a naval reserve unit on Swan Island.

"At the time, I thought 'winemakers are not farmers'; sometimes that's still the case. It never occurred to me to be a winemaker. I wasn't interested in making the commitment to the industry to make wine. I had a full-time job and a farm to run, that was enough. Besides, I "C'd" my way through science in college. My only connection to studying agriculture was walking by the Ag building - I certainly hadn't planned on being a farmer either, much less a grape grower."

He did try to convince his cherry-growing friends - in the Eola hills that grapes were a good investment, but none of them would plant.

Maresh would later comment that the grape growers were a lot more fun than the cherry growers anyway.

Early OWA meeting

Before the formation of OWA (the Oregon Winegrowers Association) winemaking was run at the county level. Erath, Dave Lett, Fuqua and I were doing things here in Yamhill County. Vulsteke, Coury, Fuller and Ponzi were doing their thing in Washington County.

Early industry meetings were held in the Tigard Firehall. No one called it the Oregon Winegrowers Association then. We were just a group of growers and potential growers meeting to talk about the Oregon wine industry.

Maresh had a rule about wine drinking - the meetings started at 7:00 p.m. and no one could start drinking until 9:00 p.m.

"Instead of adhering to my rule, Chuck Coury would stroll around the room, kibitzing and drinking wine like he was 'grand marshal'. Yea, that's Chuck. He had a strong personality, but maybe that's what the industry needed at the time."

Farmers thwart subdivision, set precedence for land-use laws.

In the mid 1960s, Allen Fruit Company of Newberg owned hundreds of acres in the Red Hills. They farmed fruit and nuts for their processing plant. Oregon's groundbreaking land-use laws were not yet in effect; there was no LCDC (Land Conservation and Development Commission, an Oregon land-use planning board).

Allen Fruit sold five-hundred acres to Standard Investment, Inc., the same five hundred acres where Knudsen-Erath was established ten years later. They continued to apply to the county to build a huge subdivision for the time, with 500 housing permits.

Maresh's neighbors, farmers John Meyer and Fred Holzmeier and I decided to oppose the builders. The three of us had farms that comprised many acres of land surrounding the proposed subdivision. We felt that dense housing would conflict with our ability to farm effectively. We all appeared before the county commissioners to appeal the building application and barely prevented the subdivision."

By 1973, the state formed LCDC and they established a 5 -7 agricultural preserve law, based on our petition. By the late 1970's all the neighbors, the Weber's, Stephen's and Archibalds, joined us in the fight.

Meeting Dick Erath

In 1969, Dick Erath came up my driveway in an old beat up BMW. He was kind of a formidable looking big guy, with these papers under his arm and I wasn't sure I was going to let him in.

He introduced himself and said something like, 'I've looked all over the West Coast for a great viticulture site and I think you're sitting on it.'

The only vineyard in Yamhill County at the time was Dave Lett's. Erath asked me if I was interested in wine grapes.

I said 'Well, I've tried everything else'.

We farmed cherries, filberts, prunes and walnuts. I was in the process of pulling out prune orchards and converting them to filberts.

I said, 'What do you need to start?'

He said, 'We'll build a greenhouse on your property and I'll get the cuttings from Wente. We'll propagate cuttings for planting.' And so we did.

Diesel greenhouse.

I went to the bank for a greenhouse loan, with an itemized list of equipment, which included budget items, including diesel, and fertilizer. The banker asked why I was building the greenhouse.

I swallowed hard and said, 'Well, we're going to grow wine grapes'.

The banker looked astonished. Then he said,

'You can't grow wine grapes in Oregon, it won't work'.

I got back, called Dick, and told him,

'Remember from now on we're calling that greenhouse my diesel greenhouse, because I took the money out of my diesel budget to fund the greenhouse.'

Kina (Erath's wife), Loie, Ted and Ferd (farm helpers) worked up there, propagating these plants. They set them out at the foot of Worden hill road on the site of our first vineyard,

So in 1970, we planted three acres total, using milk cartons. People got the word that we were putting in a viniferous vineyard, and they were stealing my plants, they took them right out of the ground. I'd see a pickup there, and by the time I could get down the hill, they were gone.

Back then, the wineries primarily wanted Riesling. They would only take your pinot noir if you had Riesling to sell. Riesling was the big thing, especially with Erath. That was what was selling in 1970.

Picking in cherry boxes

Dick had a hand press. Ted, Ferd and I were dumping the grapes into the top of the press.

I kept saying to Dick, 'Are you sure this is going to work? My banker sure doesn't think it will.'

Dick said, 'Oh yea this is going to work.'

Twenty-five years later, when Earth had his twenty-fifth year crush anniversary, we were lying under a tree looking out at the valley.

He looked around and he said, 'Jim, did you ever think that it would be this big? I mean sometimes, we didn't know what we were doing.'

I said 'Dick, now you tell me that we didn't know what we were doing? I assumed you knew. Thanks a lot.'

Nevertheless, he made wines and they were good. I began to pull prune trees and plant more grapes. At the time the price of prunes was down to about forty dollars a ton, and I was sitting on a couple hundred tons of unsold prunes. I welcomed the idea of growing a different crop.

'You think you got problems, I'm sitting on a couple hundred tons of unsold prunes,' I said to Dick.

We had obsolete orchards that needed to be pulled anyhow. If Dick wouldn't have come on the scene, we would have just pulled all the prunes and put in filberts.

I was his first grower. I grew the grapes and he made the wine at his Chehalem vineyard.

I remember Cal Knudsen came up and he was looking for grape land. He was sent by the neighbor who said there's someone planting grapes up there. So Cal and Julia Lee came up and I was in the middle of cherry harvest and had to check the weather on the television.

Loie came in and said, 'There's somebody here who wants to talk to you.'

I said, 'It'll be awhile, I've got to watch this forecast.'

So I left them waiting in the car, with Herman the German, our large, barking German Shepard circling around the doors so they couldn't get out. Poor guy.

When I finally let him in, he told me he was interested in planting grapes, and I thought, this is really an opportunity for Dick.

This is disputed in Dick's book, 'Boys up North'. I called Kina looking for Dick, who was at ChehalemVineyards. I took Knudsen's over to Chehalem Vineyards and introduced them.

Knudsen came back to our house and wanted to buy the present Erath winery site, which was for sale for about five-hundred an acre. I tried to convince him that he should buy it for three reasons; first, you have no zoning laws, at that time if you wanted to build a home, you could; second, if the farming doesn't work, you've got beautiful view property; and third, you've got timber out there.

Cal said, 'That's not timber' and looked at me like I was some city guy who didn't know anything.

As he left he gave me his card, which read, 'C. Calvert Knudsen, V.P. Weyerhaeuser.'

So that's how Knudsen got involved. He and Dick formed the winery and then eventually split, Erath retaining winery and Knudsen becoming a partner in Argyle.

I had no interest in becoming a winemaker. To really be a good winemaker, you had to be like Fred Arterberry, who I considered to be a magician.

Fred Arterberry

I couldn't get away with anything in the vineyard, because Fred lived up there. (At the time Arterberry was married to Martha Maresh, oldest daughter of Jim and Loie). He was so meticulous about the fruit and his winemaking.

When you went into Arterberry's winery in McMinnville, it was spotless. I'd come in my dirty hip boots, and he'd say, 'Boy, you're not getting through this door.'

He made incredible wine, and sparkling cider, which he sold at McMennamins. In 1982, Knights of the Vine gave him an award for the first outstanding sparkling wine produced in Oregon.

He won several gold medals. He made a 1985 Red Hills Pinot noir that the Wine Spectator rated a 95. That was the highest rating I'd ever seen for a domestically produced Pinot noir. Then one time he produced a Chardonnay that was rated top 100 wines, I think it was number 30, from the old 108 clone. If you really get that thing ripe, you can produce some wonderful Chardonnay. But boy, Fred, he had this magic touch - he had a straight palate.

Fred made wine with Maresh grapes from our first Chardonnay vineyard below our red house. He was one of the first Oregon winemakers to have a degree from UC Davis in fermentation science. With a fermentation science degree you can make beer and wine. Miller Brewing offered him a job, but he decided to go into the wine business instead. He also attended Lewis and Clark."

Ted and Ferd

I couldn't have farmed without the help from Ferd and Ted Porthe. Great guys, brothers from Iowa, they didn't have a lot. I think they didn't finish high school, but these guys were probably the best mechanics in Yamhill County. They had a knack for machinery and they were great workers.

Here's a great story about Ted: We had a vinifera plant in the ground in 1969 - called an indicator vine. We had a little garden area behind the ground where Ted lived behind the red house. We planted it to see how a vinifera vine would grow. Dick would drive by and check on it.

He came running to my door one day, exasperated, asking, 'What happened to my indicator vine?'

It turns out Ted, who was meticulous, decided that it was a weed and he rototilled it under. So our first vine didn't make it.

Ted was in his forties in 1970. Ferd was a little older. I could not have made it without them. I could take on some pretty ambitious projects because I had these two solid guys.

The Red Hills microclimate

We harvested cherries for years, which are like grapes. Our pickers were in the orchard at dawn. I had to bring them out of the orchard at about 2:00 p.m. because the stems started to get soft and I needed the stems hard for maraschino cherries. I'd call my friends who were growers in the Eola hills and say I had to pull my guys out because it was too hot. They'd still have a crew going. I couldn't pick beyond 2:00 p.m. The Van Duzer corridor is just that much cooler.

That is why these hills are such a great microclimate, because you get that flow of marine air through the corridor and then it flows south down the Eola hills and makes it cooler. It doesn't hit the Dundee hills because we have this barricade of about a thousand feet, so we were cooled off.

The other thing is out near Forest Grove, the marine air flows through the pass there and then comes up against the Dundee hills again. So we're in this little horseshoe, it's own microclimate. I was alerted to the fact that this would be a great spot to build heat units here in the summertime by cool marine air that pushes in during the afternoon.

Planting the vineyard

"The first thing we did was space 6 x 12 feet, like they do in California, 72 square feet total. The reason I went to that was because I was still farming a lot of acreage. I had big equipment. I had big tractors and crawlers. I needed a lot of room to get through my orchards. The twelve-foot spacing worked out great for me.

I wasn't overly ambitious. Other guys put in ten and twenty acres a year. We always did it so the crew - Ferd, Ted and the family could realistically do it for us. We put in maybe two, three acres a year, occasionally four. Smaller increments helped us manage the workload.

Early vineyard maintenance

You know in those days we had a real hardy sprayer. That's how we sprayed out cherries. The first year we had a mildew problem, so the second year we decided to spray for mildew. The first couple of years, I don't think we had sprayed anything. So we cranked up our cherry sprayer, I put Joey, my son, on the back of it, and I dumped sulfur in there, I think I put too much in. So I went out there and I'm driving the tractor, and Joey is covering the arc of the plant with the sprayer.

Then there was a knock on the door a few days later. Erath said, 'Jim, I can't believe what you've done to the vineyard.' The arches we sprayed turned brown, like large McDonald's arches. The rest of the leaves were green. I hadn't mixed enough water in with the sulfur."

Chicken Manure

Ted's religious day was Saturday, so I would put on sunglasses and a big hat to hide myself while I drove the chicken manure through town for fertilizing the farm soil, because the truck emitted a manure smell all through town.

The company loaded the manure, which was the texture of ready mix concrete, into the truck.

It was a hot day in July, and I had about two inches of freeboard. So here I am, driving through Newberg thinking, 'how am I going to get over the railroad tracks?'

I had to watch the one traffic light in the town, because if I had to stop, the whole thing would slosh over the cab in this type of thing. If that happens, you have to call out the fire department to wash down the streets.

Anyhow, I had this big load of manure and I saw one of those giant Greyline buses going to the Oregon coast pulled up right alongside me. I'm in the right hand lane, I always drive in the right hand lane - the people looked out and began to slam their windows shut. So I let the bus go ahead. Then, they had to stop for the railroad track, so here I am on the other side of the bus, and they're getting the full works. It was the same mad rush to shut the windows.

So I cross the railroad track, very gently, and I had so much in there, out sloshed about a wheelbarrow full right in front of the Dairy Queen. Those people are outside ordering their food from the drive-up and then this smell emanated from my truck and they all stared at me.

Then I got on the road, finally, between Newberg and Dundee, where the bus passed me for the third time, thinking 'how do we get rid of this guy?'

Another time, we picked up a load of dry chicken manure in a borrowed dump truck that Ted drove. One Sunday, right up Ninth Street where the road begins to slope up, I noticed this big layer of dried chicken manure all the way up Worden Hill Road, past Red Hills Road. I noticed everyone was out there with brooms, sweeping it off the road. Then I noticed Ted. He was so intent on driving, he wasn't aware that he had activated the dump truck mechanism and the tail gate was open. Ted had a completely empty load, going slowly up the hill.

What we did for chicken manure. That's why things are always pretty green along the road there in Dundee...

Too much manure

We had a special machine that Ted built. We could dump our manure on the machine, hook it to the tractor and dump it. When it was raining, we would dump it below the red house by the barn, so we accumulated quite a bit of it there. That was in the 1960s. In the summertime, we'd spread it around in the soil, and it disappeared.

And then we planted a chardonnay vineyard over that sight. The leaves were really big but they began to turn yellow. We got a botanist from OSU. The botanist, Dick and I stood around pondering the problem.

Finally the botanist said,

"Have you ever had chickens out here, because it show's signs of excessive nitrogen, which is found in chicken manure. The vineyard survived, but it took several years to grow out of the nitrogen residue."

First Crush 1973

When we first harvested in 1973 we finally had enough grapes to make some wine. We had no Hispanic pickers then, only people who were drawing social security and needed extra money, primarily ladies and a few unemployed people. Basically, it was hard to get your crop picked. It was nasty weather, and all I had were these elderly ladies. I thought, I'm not sure this is going to work because of the labor factor.

So those early harvests were comical because I had a bunch of ladies down there in the gully, where the vineyard was, and I almost had to winch them up the side of the slope to get them out of the mud.

I had a 1957 Volkswagen bus, and that's what I used for harvest. We eventually switched from boxes to bins, and I needed something to haul them in, so my guys took the seats out, left the driver's seat, and cut the middle of the bus out, so all we had was the engine, this platform thing, and the driver's seat. I could put a bin in there, or boxes, and I would haul them up to Erath, and he would unload. It was perfect. We would go right to the vineyard and pick it up.

I was telling this to a VW dealer in Albany, and he said, 'that's a great story, I'd like to use it in my national newsletter.'

Inside the letter was a picture of this beat-up 1957 Volkswagen bus up at Erath's small winery. The caption read, 'the beauty of this is when old 57 runs out of gas, we just throw a little bit of Pinot in the tank and it takes right off.'

So, during our first crush we picked six tons of grapes - the average today is about half that. From a farmer's perspective, you're going for tonnage with other crops, but not grapes. Now we now that quality, not quantity is what makes a great wine. High-yield, low-density.

Well, Dick had a television crew out at the winery filming a segment on harvesting.

I was running behind Dick yelling in excitement, 'Hey we're getting six tons an acre' and he's in front of the camera explaining that we're going for quality, not quantity, and shooting me dirty looks.

At the time, I wasn't much of a red wine drinker - I liked a good Riesling, which sold for about four hundred dollars a ton back then. The public liked Riesling too, they were accustomed to drinking sweeter white wines, and there's nothing wrong with that. It also went on the market faster than red wine, which requires more aging and tending.

We had parties after harvesting, where we made up skits about each other. For one skit, Dick was dressed as a king, the holy winemaker - and Arthur and I were in rags, the poor, humble, grape growers. Arthur and I got on our knees as we offered him a crate of grapes, beseeching him to pay us top dollar. He would look at the grapes and yell 'rejected' and bang a big gong, at which point Arthur and I collapsed into agony on the ground.

We competed to see who could write the best script, which we judged on applause from the crowd. I won for two years running. The third year the group decided to form a conspiracy against me, but I saw it coming. They were sitting around the dining room table, voting on the skits, and I had to leave the room when they voted on mine. Little did they know that the night before, in preparation for their plot, I had my children cheer and applaud loudly into a tape recorder, which I stashed in my room.

When the group sent me out, they solemnly brought my name up for voting, and no one clapped on purpose. They thought they had me. All of the sudden, I flipped on my tape recorder from the other room, with the volume up. They jumped straight out of their chairs...

The ups and downs of growing grapes

Grapes, like any crop, have good harvest years and bad harvest years. During the famous disastrous harvest of 1984 we had 17 inches of rain in one month. One harvest, the weather was so cold my Riesling refused to ripen. I finally got it to seventeen brix, well under the twenty-two that it should have been

The winemaker who was buying the grapes said, 'just bring it in and we'll try to do something with it.'

So, I put the crates on the truck and they were at seventeen brix. I drove through the rain, halfway down the highway, and they were down to fifteen brix, they'd dropped two brix just on the drive - it was a disaster.

Another time I lost ten-thousand dollars worth of cherries with one rain, which split the skins. We're not like California, where every year is the same weather.

Grape growing advice:

Grape growing is hard on marriages. Both parties have to make a commitment to growing grapes or making wine. If one doesn't want to do it, it doesn't work. This industry is a graveyard for marriages.

Have a contract to sell your grapes. This business is cyclical. We're in an oversupply situation right now. Make sure you have someone to buy your product.

Expect a seven-year program before full production. Develop a farm plan. Remember, one out of five years are substandard or sheer disaster years.

To sell more wine in your tasting room get the winemaker and vineyard manager to walk through the tasting room. Everyone wants to know how you grow the grapes. When you explain these details, take them in the vineyard, I sold a lot of wine out of the Red Barn.

The one thing I hope we never lose is our small wineries. None of us expected to have this be anything but a way of life - I'd like to see the continuation of that. Small, boutique wineries, different from California, more friendly.

Martha Maresh:

"The farm is my home," said Martha Maresh. She's helped in the daily farm and vineyard operations since she was old enough to prune and water.

Martha planted vines when she was five-months pregnant with her only child, Jimmy Arterberry. There is little downtime when you're maintaining a vineyard, physical labor is a requirement nearly year-round.

Martha walked everywhere in those early years, and continues to do the same today. She remembers early morning walks to work in neighboring vineyards watching the sunrise over the Red Hills. Besides working in her own vineyard, she worked in the vineyard's of neighbors Gary Fuqua and Dick Erath, where she also eventually managed the tasting room.

As Martha fondly recalls, clothing was occasionally optional in the vineyard in those days. With no one else for miles around, she would tie grapes au naturale and enjoy being outside. She wasn't the only local who practiced this art.

In the 1980s, she and her late husband, Fred Arterberry, along with Fred's parents, operated Arterberry Winery in McMinnville.

Martha remarried in the mid 1990s. She still manages the farm and retreat center with her father and family.

She credits her mother and all the other women in the wine industry for being stellar role models and equal partners in the success of grape growing.

"The women were equally marketing, promoting and doing everything the men were doing, just not getting as much credit for it. They were as much involved as the men planting, harvesting and pruning," said Martha.

Bill and Bessie Archibald
Archibald Vineyards

The Archibald's purchased twenty acres in the Dundee Hills on Worden Hill Road in 1971 and lived there until 1988. They planted five acres in vineyard and built a house. The vineyard is now owned and operated by Archery Summit.

"It was a long way from South Africa to Dundee, but we were struck by the bug, by the romance of wine," recalled Bessie Archibald.

Bessie and Bill, native Canadians, had lived in Montréal, South Africa and Portland while they raised their family. Bill was a mechanical engineer. He specialized in steam and recovery operations in pulp and paper mills.

"At that time there were only three sets of lights along Worden Hill Road, ours, Maresh's and Nita Moyer's," recalled Bessie, "Yet here was this burgeoning wine industry in the middle of a Quaker community."

Newberg, the town next to Dundee was founded by Quakers, who are strict teetotalers. Until the late 1970s, Newberg was a 'dry' town – no liquor store or bars that sold hard liquor.

The Archibald's were drawn to the Dundee hills after visiting their former Portland neighbors, the Medici's, during the late 1960s at the Medici's home in Newberg. The Medici's were also planting a vineyard. The Archibald's found some land they liked along Worden Hill Road and introduced themselves to Jim Maresh, whose land bordered the acreage they were considering buying.

When the Archibald's consulted with Maresh about what they should farm; Maresh's reply was, naturally, 'plant a vineyard!'

By then Jim's enthusiasm for vineyards was palpable.

"Talking to him for five minutes was really all you needed to convince yourself that planting a vineyard was the best thing that you could do in your lifetime, and maybe the next. He left out the backbreaking labor part, but he could be forgiven for that," Bessie recalled.

The family purchased the acreage and began the tedious task of planting their vineyard. Bill went to work everyday, while Bessie managed the family, house and farm. She also drove the tractor, rototilled and farmed as assiduously as her husband.

"It was twenty acres of blackberries and poison oak" she recalled. The acreage had been farmed as strawberry fields in the early part of the century by the Herring family.

The Archibald's twenty acres were separate from the original Herring farmhouse and land. They constructed their own house in 1972.

From the start, the Archibalds were welcomed by their Red Hills neighbors, who helped with support, advice and food. The day the family moved in, Loie Maresh showed up with a huge picnic basket of food to eat amidst the moving boxes.

"She fed people," recalls Bessie.

In what is now infamous Red Hills lore, the Archibald's were soon to discover that the Maresh's were prepared to offer more than just food and advice.

The overland vineyard project.

Somehow, the Archibald's contractor had neglected to install the last 20 feet of pipe in their newly dug well, so the pipe failed to reach the water; consequently they were temporarily without water for their new house and vineyard.

"Let's hook you up," said Jim Maresh, who continued, along with Arthur Weber and Bill Archibald, to run an irrigation pipe all the way from Maresh's well at the top of the ridge above the Archibald's new vineyard.

"This was not a couple of yards of irrigation pipe, I guess it was at least a mile," recalled Jim Maresh.

Armed with PVC cement for the pipe and connectors and a machete for the blackberries, the threesome hacked their way through the brush and red dirt to lay the pipe.

"We had to work for a week measuring black plastic tubes. We rolled miles of tubes out trying to get it all in place," Daughter Shawna recalled,

Finally, they connected the pipe from Maresh's well to Archibald's property.

"We all stood around at the top of the pipe by the pump waiting for the water to come out for the first time. First it was a trickle, then we heard it gushing, next thing we knew, about 10 yards away, the pipe exploded and a wall of water flew into the air, soaking Arthur. We had some refining to do," recalled Jim Maresh.

That first year, Bill studied viticulture and went to a course taught by local wine legend Charles Coury at Portland Community College.

"Functionality was beauty to Bill. He wanted to know how everything worked," said Bessie.

She said he always loved to exercise and work in the vineyard but also developed a passion for tractors. He owned three of them. He prided himself on his driving skills - a competitive sport in the hills.

"One day Bill got stuck in the ravine that I always had a bad feeling about," remembered Bessie. "He was irritated that he couldn't get out. His tires were sunk in the mud. Finally, admitting defeat, he walked over to Maresh's and asked for help."

He couldn't find Jim, but he did find one of Maresh's vineyard helpers, Ferd, after he'd walked at least a mile through the dirt and heat.

Ferd pulled him out with a tractor more powerful than his, a story Ferd recalled with delight throughout his lifetime.

Planting the vineyard:

The Archibald's, like several other early growers, bought grape starts from Coury, who ran a nursery whose motto was 'propagators of noble wine grapes.' He sold three different kinds of cuttings including twenty-three kinds of vinifera, fourteen hybrids and six root stock varieties.

Coury's vinifera list printed on his nursery pamphlet included the following extensive variety: Aligote, Barbera, Cabernet Franc, Cabernet Sauvignon, Chardonnay, Chenin Blanc, Gamay Beaujolais, Gamay noir, Gewurtraminer, Malbec, Merlot, Meunier, Muller Thurgau, Pinot Blanc, Pinot Gris, Pinot noir, Petite Syrah, Petite Verdon, Sauvignon Blanc, Semillon, Sylvaner, White Riesling and Zinfandel.

"We had this bizarre blend of clones. We got a paper bag with tiny starts in it; a strange, unknown mix of clones and varietals from the Coury nursery." recalled Shawna.

Coury's famous 'Paper bag' stock was described in his pamphlet as 'a 2 ½ x 6 inch deep Japanese paper pot container. Roots penetrate container wall. Plant pot, vine and all.'

Clearly, keeping rootstock separated was a problem faced by many growers.

The Archibald's concentrated on the same grape stock as other growers in the hills, Pinot noir, Chardonnay and Riesling.

"Pommard stock, according to Coury," said Bessie.

In 1972, the same year they built the house, the family planted between four and five acres of vineyards on the top of the hill behind it.

By 1980, the Archibalds's acreage blended into an almost three-mile strip of undulating hills with vineyards bordering Worden Hill Road. But when they first planted it, overgrown orchards and blackberries dominated the view from the road.

Vineyard work

While plotting the vineyard, the daughters strung miles of cord throughout the house, measuring off the rows, in a chaotic mess.

Besides plotting the original rows, Shawna and Claire helped plant, water and maintain the original vines.

When the family was establishing the vineyard, the sisters recall planting the cuttings and filling the milk cartons that surrounded them with water from the hose. They also hoed. As the vines matured, they pruned, tied and picked.

Bill Archibald once knocked himself out, literally, while driving posts into the ground with a posthole driver. The heavy metal driver, shaped like a soup pot with handles on both sides, is used by inserting the post-hole driver over the top of the stake. Then, you grasp both handles, lift up and pull down with as much force as possible. After a couple of repetitions, the momentum and weight drives the stake into the ground. It was backbreaking, slow work. Somehow, Bill accidentally hit himself on the side of the head and passed out. Bessie found him in the vineyard, with a bloody cut on the side of his head.

She asked him, "How long have you been out?"

He replied, "I don't know."

Despite this temporary setback, Bill determinedly drove more stakes until the hillside was dotted with poles and trellising like a great green pincushion.

Shawna had always wanted to live in the country and have a horse. When they moved to the vineyard, she bought a horse and named it Rebel. She enjoyed riding Rebel on old logging trails in the hills with her former neighbor, Nancy Medici.

She also rode often through the vineyards; once she looked down and noticed a coin where the horse had scraped the mud away. She jumped off the horse, picked it up and realized that it was an 1866 silver dollar.

Bessie also recalled that there were stressful times when they were establishing the vineyard; between money, time and labor needs. Shawna credits Paul Hart and Rex Hill Vineyard Management for bringing the growers stability in the mid 1980s. At last, they could have some assurance that their crop would be purchased.

"After all, it really took about ten years for these vineyards to get established. That's a long investment for an uncertain payoff. Two weeks before harvest a winemaker might say he didn't need your grapes after all, and then what do you do with them?" said Bessie.

Bill and Julia Wayne:
Abbey Ridge Vineyards, Cameron Winery

Bill and Julia first arrived in Oregon in 1975. They purchased fifty-two acres in the Red Hills in 1977 and planted their original acreage. The couple has three children, Phoebe, Jenny and Ian. They co-established Cameron winery in 1984 in the Red Hills with winemaker Jon Paul and his wife, Teri Wadsworth, and Shawna Archibald and Marc Dochez.

"We wanted a different experience," said Julia when she recalled why they planted grape vines on an Oregon hillside.

Bill Wayne and Julia Stuart met as seniors at Whitman College. Bill majored in biology, Julia in art.

Dundee 1979: Bill and Julia Wayne on their front porch

Bill Wayne harvesting grapes

Bill had been working on a large wheat ranch, where he drove bean combines, wheat trucks, built fences (sometimes known as 'cowboy carpentry') and generally learned agricultural skills. The pay was $2.50 an hour.

Julia recalls sitting at the kitchen table around that time with fellow friend and Whitman graduate Marc Dochez, thinking about what they were going to do with their lives.

Bill and Julia visited friends in Oregon in 1975. The friends of the newly married couple, who were then working in the local restaurant industry, at a Portland restaurant called L'auberge, encouraged the couple to explore Oregon wines. At the time, Bill was en route to UC Davis to study viticulture. The couple were intrigued by the idea, but continued on to Davis to learn more about wine before deciding where to settle.

At Davis, Bill studied viticulture techniques, but also developed some theories and idea of his own, through independent reading and interviewing. He decided that Davis was serving the California wine industry. The Davis growing methodology was really designed for growers with huge acreages like Taylor and Cribari in Southern California who were large-scale wine producers making generic 'table wine'.

Although upscale wineries were flourishing in parts of Northern California, Gallo and the other large producers still basically set prices for all the growers.

Bill decided he wanted to grow quality grapes on lush hillsides. He read Charles Coury's thesis on cold climate growing. He read about Burgundy. He decided that Oregon was where he really wanted to be.

"In Oregon it looked like something you could do on a small acreage - twenty or forty acres," Bill recalled. "Land in Napa was at least ten to twenty-thousand dollars an acre. Gallo controlled the price of most grapes in California, at the time they paid three-hundred dollars a ton. There was more opportunity in Oregon."

During spring break during his year at Davis, Bill called Charles Coury, David Lett and Dick Erath and arranged to meet them to discuss how to plant a vineyard in Oregon. They encouraged him to come on up.

Bill and Julia arrived at Charles Coury's house, where they were greeted with an intense discussion about UC Davis.

Bill Wayne recalled his discussion with Coury that day, "Coury discussed UC Davis curriculum and commented, 'you just sat there and let them tell you that crap?' and I wasn't really offended because I knew he was a brilliant guy. He told me to read his thesis, just like he told everyone else, and he knew what he was talking about."

Julia's mother, Barbara Stuart, had called it when she told the couple, "You guys ought to grow grapes."

These fortuitous meetings helped the Wayne's form a plan – they decided to go to Oregon and start a vineyard.

"We were intrigued by the idea of growing wine grapes in Oregon," said Julia. "We were fortunate that we had our parents behind us. Our parents helped us with the initial startup costs. It was so outside of what my father was interested in. It seemed like a risk to him, but we were too dumb to care. We made up for lack of knowledge with confidence," said Julia.

Buying the Land

The Wayne's credit David Lett, Dick Erath, Charles Coury, and Jim McDaniel for helping in the early years of their vineyard dream.

Julia recalled working in the Eyrie vineyard when they first came to Oregon in 1975, on an Easter Sunday, all alone, working outside on a beautiful sunny day. It was idyllic.

In 1977, the Wayne's moved from UC Davis to Oregon in their Volvo wagon, towing a Uhaul full of firewood that they had hauled from Walla Walla, through Oregon to Davis and back to Oregon again.

Their first home in Oregon was on Dr. Tom Gail's farm in Newberg, where the couple helped around the farm.

They continued to pursue their dream, working and learning as much as possible in David Lett's, Gary Fuqua's and other vineyards.

Bill wanted to sell grapes to David Lett, whom he considered a talented winemaker. They looked at land in the Eola hills, Tualatin and Elk Cove, but kept circling the Dundee hills.

In 1978, they moved into the Knudsen cabin above the Knudsen Erath winery and continued to look for vineyard land. One day in early fall, Dick Erath suggested that they look over the hill, on Worden hill road at one-hundred and fifty acres for sale as a possible vineyard site.

In a rush, the Wayne's hurried over the hill, parked, and crashed through the underbrush and blackberries down to the freshly tilled slope of prime vineyard acreage with a breathtaking view of the valley. At the time, Larry Wade, a local farmer, was farming the acreage for the owner.

"The soil looked like cake. It was almost surreal. We had stars in our eyes," recalled Julia. The picture perfect scene ended at the bottom of the ravine, where four grown and one baby elk stood grazing quietly, watching the couple.

They were so excited about the property that Bill jumped in the car and insisted that the realtor walk the boundaries of the land. Grudgingly, the realtor, accompanied by an enthusiastic Bill, waded through the underbrush and trees around the perimeter of the property and established the boundaries.

That year, they bought fifty-two acres out of the original approximately one-hundred fifty acre parcel. They moved out of the cabin and bought a small, spartan trailer, which they moved onto the land.

Living in the trailer, building house:

They lived on the land in a trailer while they were planting the vineyard and building the house. In May of 1978, Marc Dochez came for six weeks and stayed for six months, offering his carpentry services. He and Bill built the house themselves.

"It was a magical time. Marc gave us six months of his life. It was quite a gift," said Julia.

They moved out of the trailer when the mice got too noisy, onto the front porch of the semi-constructed house. The outdoor bedroom for the rest of the summer consisted of their bed, a rocking chair, and their first child Phoebe's crib.

Under the light of kerosene lamps, they moved in that fall, without electricity, although they did have a well, running water, and one toilet with a curtain for a door. They were used to living in little houses in the country; they'd been living off of the land for years.

"If we could scrape together the materials, we could do it," said Julia. She remembered that once they had gathered hundreds of pounds of apples and made gallons of apple cider.

"It was big romantic game," said Julia. She added, however, that it was not fun to live so close to the land when they had their baby.

Everything revolved around the woodpile. To make the house warm she had to put the baby down and run to the woodpile for firewood. When she wanted to cook, again she had to run to the woodpile to start the stove.

They had a line for electricity, but it didn't work right away. She remembered thinking, "This is really, ridiculous. I live in twentieth century, not the nineteenth. I need a dishwasher and a real stove."

Planting the Vineyard

They planted the first vineyard on two acres at the top slope of the property, for maximum exposure to the sun. They used lime-coated foot-long marking sticks to mark the plants, in preparation for full stakes with wire to come.

They went to bed that evening, and woke up early in the morning. They eagerly looked out the window at the vineyard, but couldn't see the stakes - the only thing out there looked like chewed toothbrush bristles. Although the elk walked through the young vineyard plantings without eating them, they hadn't been able to resist the lime-dipped stakes.

They used bean poles, bean wire and got a really good deal on some used electrical wire. Bill's cowboy carpentry skills learned in his Whitman days were put to test when he had to stop every fifty feet and untangle the wire.

The Wayne's used cuttings from Fuqua, Lett and Erath. They nurtured them at a friend's nursery hotbed.

During one of their first harvests

Bill would get up early in the morning to chase the birds out of the vines with dogs Arlie and Irving and a shotgun. He'd start running and waving his arms at the top of the hill, or fire a shotgun into the sky, making as much noise as possible, to ward off the birds who were trying to eat the ripe fruit. Often he'd spend hours running up and down the vineyard slope. Julia felt sorry for him and spelled him occasionally.

Bill remembered another grower, Preston Vineyards, losing an entire crop to birds, and he did not want to suffer the same fate.

Mt. St. Helens ash was still covering the vines the day they decided to harvest their first crop. Their shoulders covered in fine grey ash, they picked fifteen boxes of grapes with Marc Dochez and Shawna Archibald.

They say there were some low points after that, but not many. The fruit rotted on the vine another year, and occasionally they worried about finding buyers for their crop.

"We were foolishly confident, but it worked out," says Julia.

Bill believed from the beginning that this was a viable industry. He studied soil maps and decided that Jory soil, our red soil in the hills, was the best choice."

Cameron Winery

The Wayne's still own the original vineyard property, which is now planted with twenty acres of Pinot noir.

They are co-owners of Cameron winery. Cameron's winemaker John Paul, like the Wayne's and many others in the early vineyard years, lived in the Erath cabin when he first came to Oregon in 1978. He helped with some early crushes in the vineyards, and brought back some grapes to test in the Carneros region of California, where he had been making wine. He sent back a positive report, and decided that Oregon was the place he wanted to make wine.

The Wayne's, Marc Dochez, Shawna Archibald and John Paul, with his wife Terri, formed a partnership and established Cameron winery in 1983. John has made award-winning wines from the Wayne's vineyard, and other Oregon grapes.

"It's a good family business," said Julia.

WINDERLEA VINEYARDS AND WINERY
BILL SWEAT AND DONNA MORRIS.
Bill Sweat and Donna Morris relocated from Boston in 2006 and founded Winderlea Winery.

They built a modern winery facility and have crafted premium Pinot Noir and Chardonnay from their 20 acres of vineyards, including the vineyard they purchased from the Bauer family, since 2008.

Their 2012 vintage prominently features Pommard, Dijon 115, Wadenswil and Coury Clone Pinot noir produced from the 35 year-old former Bauers vineyard.

Dr. John and Sally Bauers:
Red Hills Vineyard
John Bauers, originally from Latvia, and Sally Bauers, originally from Kansas, purchased fifteen acres of a historic filbert farm in 1974. They bought an additional five acres of planted vineyard from Jim McDaniel in the mid 1970s and another five acres from the Jones family that included a house. They planted fifteen total acres of grapes and sold to various wineries for three decades. The family moved into the house the day Mt. St Helens blew up. "It helped the crop" said Sally.

"Something about the hills gets in your blood. There is no other place like it in the world." recalled Sally Bauers.

John Bauers, enjoyed working in his grandfather's fruit winery with his grandfather when he was a child in Ranka, Latvia during the 1930s. He never forgot how much he liked to harvest, press the fruit, distill and bottle the wine. Decades later in the late 1960s, he planted a small vineyard in his backyard in Oak Grove, Oregon where he lived with Sally and their three children.

It was in Oak Grove that they met and hired Francis, their gardener who eventually became their first and only vineyard manager.

In 1973, a family friend gave the Bauers a bottle of Oregon Spring Wine, which was a mixture of red and white grapes made by David Lett of Eyrie Vineyards. They were intrigued by the taste and the smell of one of Oregon's first wines.

"We'd never had anything like it before. Immediately John was taken with the idea of growing grapes on a hillside to make wine like that," said Sally.

"We have to go find a southwest facing slope," declared John, who was convinced that hillside vineyards produced better fruit than valley farming.

They drove all over Yamhill County for a year and a half looking for vineyard acreage. The family knew the drill: make a picnic, drive around looking for realty signs, stop and eat the picnic at some scenic area in the county.

In 1974, driving up and down Worden hill road, they noticed acreage that was planted in filberts beside Archibald and Weber Vineyards Although it had no realty sign, the couple knew they had found the property.

They bought the fifteen acres and continued to live in Oak Grove until daughter Liz graduated from high school. They also bought a five-acre vineyard on the other side of the road from Jim McDaniel.

John continued to work at his medical practice as an osteopathic physician, and managed the vineyard in the evenings.

"John had so much energy; he needed to work two jobs. Besides, he was terrible at golf," said Sally. "The vineyard was his mid-life crisis, which I considered better than a woman. Come to think of it, there were many middle-aged men up in the hills that choose the vineyard as their 'mid-life crisis'."

Planting the Vineyard

When John met his neighbor, Bill Archibald, he instantly recognized him. They had both recently taken a class from Charles Coury about viticulture in Oregon at Portland Community College.

Bessie invited Sally to use the oven for casseroles so they would have something to eat while they planted their vineyard.

Family, friends and Francis started planting the first five acres of vines in 1974, after installing an outhouse. They planted the second five later on that summer, and finished planting the rest in the summer of 1975.

John laid out the vineyard and Francis drove the stakes. Then the family formed a crew and established an assembly line.

"First, Francis dug the hole for the plant, then Liz followed with a one-third cup of fertilizer, which she poured in each hole. Following Liz was Dana, who dropped the plant by the hole. Next, John Jr. planted the cutting, and the rest of us came behind and pushed the dirt around. It was a wonderful family experience. Our children felt like they had some ownership of the property," recalled Sally.

Of course, child labor laws were not what they are today so the children brought their junior high and high school friends out to work with them. They worked and played simultaneously. Sally recalls that the neighborhood kids loved to work in the vineyard, loved to be outside in the fresh air, and liked the work better than strawberry picking. Often, she'd have to turn down children because there wasn't enough room to take them all.

"We'd take as many kids as could fit into the van and drive them out to work in the vineyard for the day. We even had a woman from John's office staff, her husband and their children help plant the vineyard that summer," recalled Sally.

I said, "Why would you want to do this?" and they replied "We've never planted a vineyard before, so why not?"

In their upper vineyard, the family finished planting the 75% completed vineyard with Pinot gris vines.

"Riesling and the Pinot gris thrived in the upper vineyard. Those grapes made fabulous wine," said Sally.

The Bauer's, like many others, bought their rootstock from Charles Coury.

"He was a great salesman and a great winemaker. Everyone went to Coury for their root stock," said Sally

On the fifteen acres, they planted Wadenswil clone Pinot noir, Chardonnay, Riesling, Cabernet and a few rows of Merlot, which Sally said aged beautifully on the lower southern slope because of the heat - "it got baked." However, unlike the other varietals, the Merlot yielded a very small crop of fruit, so they eventually took it out.

"Elk Cove made some wonderful wine with our Merlot, unfortunately, the yield was so low per acre we had to replace it," said Sally.

They bought an additional five acres and moved into their house the day Mt. St. Helens blew up.

"You know, the vineyard really thrived later that summer after the eruption. We noticed the leaves were vibrant and the fruit rich from the ash," said Sally.

The Bauers' oldest daughter, Dana, worked in the vineyard with Francis to earn college money in the summer. At the end of the day, Francis took her to Alice's for a cheeseburger.

"John and I had a pact with each other. If either of us started talking about how nice it might be to have our own winery, we'd slap each other. I mean, you get the 'fever' sometimes. One of us would get that look in our eye, and say, 'oh, it'd be so lovely to make wine' while in reality we knew that it was incredibly hard work. Growing grapes was hard enough," laughed Sally.

The family pruned, suckered, tied and harvested grapes alongside Francis and the occasional vineyard crews.

Winemaking

When the vineyard reached maturity and began producing in the early 1980s, the Bauer's sold their crop to Elk Cove, Erath, Eyrie, Rex Hill and Lange winery. They grew commercial grapes but also make some of their own wine in their basement from their own harvest.

"John was a great amateur winemaker, but he was too modest to ever enter his wine in any contests," said Sally.

They built a room in the basement, under the deck, to use as their home winery. While they still lived in Oak Grove, they'd bought a wine press from an elderly Italian woman, whose husband had made wine with it since the depression.

"Everyone wanted to buy our grapes after they'd tasted John's Cabernet and Pinot. He'd go down in the basement a pop a bottle for guests. By the end of the bottle, the grapes in the vineyard were sold," said Sally.

Grape buying 'etiquette' usually requires that the buyer start inquiring about purchasing the grapes in June, even though harvest isn't until September or October. Or, at least you try to have them sold by early summer.

Harvesting

As Sally recalled, Francis usually 'did everything' during harvest. John also built a weighing scale for the totes, so they could weigh them before they sent the fruit to the wineries, (payment is by the ton). Francis kept track of all the weights, drove the tractor, and kept everything on track. He also delivered occasional totes to the family winery, then dumped the fruit in the press.

Sally filled two picnic tables with food during harvest. She fed the crowd, whether they were working in the vineyard or just watching the crew.

1984 Harvest

The harvest of 1984 was one of the worst on record for winegrowers. Torrents of rain created slippery, muddy hillsides that were almost impossible to navigate. Fruit rotted on the vine.

John Bauers attended a board of medical examiner's meeting and left Sally and Francis in charge of the harvest.

"I'll never forget that year. It was a nightmare for everybody," said Sally. Francis and Sally stood ankle deep in mud, cutting rain ponchos out of garbage bags for the water sodden crew.

Real disaster almost struck when Sally was driving her Chevrolet Silverado, already in 4 wheel drive, down the upper vineyard hillside. She touched the brakes, and the car didn't slow down. It started skidding, then turned sideways and kept sliding, straight toward Worden Hill road. Right at the edge of a ten-foot embankment, precariously close to the edge, the car stopped.

"Other than the occasional crisis, it was a great family experience. I wouldn't trade it for the world," recalled Sally.

Gary and Saundra Fuqua:
Fuqua Vineyards/Erath Grower

The Fuqua's bought thirty-five acres in 1971 and built a house on the acreage. Deb and Bill Hatcher, owners of Rex Hill and A to Z winery, rented the basement of the house when they first moved to Oregon to work at Domaine Drouhin in the late 1980s.

Gary Fuqua is one of the few native Oregonians' to plant a vineyard in the Red Hills. He attended Cleveland high school. His sister, Linda, was a Rose Festival queen.

His interest in wine began at around age 21, when he traveled for four months through Europe and sampled wines from Burgundy, Alsace and Bordeaux.

After working as an economist for the Army Corps of Engineers in Seattle and Washington DC, Gary returned to his native state and purchased thirty-five acres of land in the Dundee Hills. He explored vineyard sites in Roseburg, and spoke to David Lett and Dick

Left to right: Gary, Eric, Saundra, Jason and Paige Fuqua 1972

Erath, who both had land in the Red Hills. They encouraged him to plant vines in the rich soil. That year, he built a house on the property and prepared the vineyard site.

He soaked beanpoles in creosote to use for stakes, then strung the traditional four-wire trellising system and installed cedar stakes for end posts. In 1977, after traveling to the Alsace and Burgundy wine regions in France and Germany with Dick Erath, he first saw and later installed a catch wire system in the vineyard.

Gary took short courses at UC Davis in viticulture and enology to increase his vineyard knowledge.

He cleared the land and tilled the vineyard site with a 1965 Massey Ferguson tractor, then planted three acres of Pinot noir and Riesling from two clones, Wadenswil and Gamay noir. He ordered the Pinot noir rootstock from Carl Wente nursery in Livermore, California and purchased the Riesling from Coury.

The company delivered the rootstock from California late in June, when it was already warm. He struggled to keep the cuttings alive and lost "quite a few." The next year he persevered and by 1986, he had twenty acres of Pinot noir, Chardonnay, Pinot gris and Riesling.

Like other growers, Gary did the majority of the work, spraying, pruning and rotatilling in his vineyard himself, although he hired crews and his children to help tie and harvest the vines.

Harvesting

Fuqua's first wine sale was to Dick Erath in 1975. Throughout the years, he also sold to Sokol-Blosser, Adelsheim, Yamhill Valley, Lange and Argyle.

Gary has consistently sold his grapes every year. He has never had to leave grapes on the vine. He noted that in the 1970s, there was more variation in the fruit, more extreme factors – rot and weather exposure often affected entire vintages. 1977 and 1984 were notably bad harvests.

Gary noticed the factors that sell the grapes have changed since the early years. Growers sold their grapes on contract based almost exclusively on the sugar level of the fruit, anywhere from eighteen to twenty-three brix. Now, the growing emphasis is on crop level and yield, striving to attain concentrated fruit and good acid level. Cool summer nights in Oregon help the fruit ripen slowly and develop the acidity needed.

Winemaking

Gary made thirty to forty gallons of wine in his basement until the early 1980s. For one of his first winemaking attempts, he borrowed a press from Bill Blosser to get the juice. He used the same methods other home winemaker's employed, carboys and lab tubing in the basement.

Their daughter, Paige Fuqua Richardson, was four-years old when they bought the land.

"My earliest memories are of milk cartons all over the hillside with little cuttings in them. We all planted it, semi-willingly, but my dad was the driving force behind it all. He believed in the dream. I remember watching him drive the tractor after work in the dark and working with him watering on weekends trying to keep everything alive," recalled Paige.

Paige and her brothers' first jobs' were working in the vineyard. They tied, suckered and harvested in the fall. Their dad paid them one dollar, twenty-five cents an hour, which they considered good money for teenage jobs in the late 1970s.

They tied the vines to the wires with little twisties from Glad bags.

"Now they take a big net and throw it over the vineyard to train the vines. Back then, all we had were the twisties," said Paige.

Depending on the season, she recalled the red mud was either dusty or muddy in the rows.

"I'll never forget the feeling of red mud crusted on my boots, slogging through ankle deep wet soil. All my clothes were stained with red dirt. You sacrificed most of your clothing to the vineyard," said Paige.

Her father bought her two horses, Freckles and Tina. She rode all over the hills, and even helped in the vineyard during early harvest, before the grapes were ready to pick.

"We'd set our bird cannons out and I would ride up and down the rows turning them off or on. If we were close to them and they went 'boom', Freckles would take off running down the row. You held on to the horse or you were walking back to the house. It was not an easy job."

She's now married to her junior high school sweetheart, and remembered riding bareback through the vineyard with him as 'very romantic.'

She also recalled that living on a vineyard was an agricultural experience, and not always a safe one. She remembered that one time the gophers were eating the roots of the young grapes and digging large mounds in the freshly plowed rows. Her father was so disgusted with the gophers that he laid out poison gopher pellets in the rows.

Another time, her grandfather fell into the steep blackberry patch rimming the hillside of the vineyard. He completely disappeared into the blackberries as the family waded in to fish him out.

"It was awful, like a horror movie - attack of the blackberries. We were covered in blackberries and blood from blackberry vine thorns, but we did manage to rescue granddaddy and ourselves," said Paige.

She recalls vivid memories of vineyard life during harvest, "I remember harvest parties at Erath's every year, with the music of the Police blaring and us dancing. We were so happy to be done working in the vineyard all day."

She recalled the early morning hours during harvest, when she awoke before sunrise to work in the vineyard before it was too warm. The warm, dusty smell of ripe grapes on the vine always brings back two memories for her.

"I will always remember eating grapes until I was sick, every harvest. Nothing tastes as good as a fully ripe wine grape, and nothing will give you a worse stomach ache if you eat too much of them, kind of like the hangover without the alcohol," said Paige.

"Also during harvest we had dirt clod fights and grape fights. We'd grab a cluster and race up to someone's turned back, and splat, throw the ripe bunch at their back or stuff it down their shirt, then run away. The only drawback when you're running away is that those rows can be awfully long with no exit," she recalled.

Her father was an innovator, like many other growers. Tired of separating the leaves of branches from his filbert crop, he developed a filbert-sorting machine made of chicken wire, wood and a large metal tray.

"You could dump them in the tray and they came out sorted. He was so proud of that thing. He should have patented it," said Paige.

Gary Fuqua harvesting grapes in Fuqua Vineyards 1979.

Fuqua's winery was in their basement. He primarily sold his tonnage to Dick Erath, but kept some for himself to make his own wine.

Paige recalled her father's bottles in the bathtub, where he soaked old labels off California wine bottles and sterilized them with detergent.

She remembered that he made wine with a little press in the basement cellar and occasional bottled in the basement laundry room. There were bottles everywhere, and laundry.

"It was like a mad science laboratory," said Paige. The vintage 1976 Pinot noir bottles were mixed in the shelves with canned goods and folded clothes."

She added, "During harvest, I remember standing on a slightly damp, sticky, wine-soaked floor loading the laundry. The smell of musty fermenting grapes permeated any clothing that came out of the dryer, and fruit flies buzzed around my head. I remember thinking that this is not a normal laundry room."

Fuqua's was one of first Oregon vineyard's with phylloxera. The original plantings were eventually pulled out and replaced with stronger virus resistant stock by Archery Summit. In 1980, he sold ten acres to Alan and Sally Holstein. In 1993, he sold the original twenty-five acres to Archery Summit.

Russell Fuqua, Gary's father, owned acreage adjacent to Gary's original site, which Gary helped plant in pinot noir. He bought the remaining vineyard property from his father in 1998 and built a house beside it.

Julia Staigers and Gerard Koschal
Juliard Vineyards, Crumbled Rock Winery

Julia Staigers and Gerard Koschal met at Wright State University in Ohio in the 1970s. In 1987, after their three girls had grown up, they decided to move to Oregon and buy a vineyard. It was the start of a new adventure in a bucolic country neighborhood for Gerry, a geologist, and Julia, an accountant.

Gerry recalled that Loie Maresh walked over with a fresh box of pears as he was standing on the property contemplating whether or not to buy it.

"If you buy this house it's a party house and you'll have to throw neighborhood parties. We like to have parties around here," said Loie.

That cinched the deal for Gerry.

They named the vineyard Juilard, after each other and replaced, with the exception of Riesling, the rest of the existing vineyard with Pinot Noir. They had to pull out the remains of an orchard, a pig sty and a rabbit hutch, which was no small feat. Like their neighbors, creating quality pinot noir from the Jory soil was their vision.

The couple's first official buyer was Bill Heron from a Rogue Valley, they also sold to Myron Redford of Amity Vineyards, Tempest Winery and Randall Graham (self-described "The Rhone Ranger"). From 1997 - 2006 they had a vineyard contract with Dick Erath, who bottled the pinot noir labeled with the Juliard Vineyard designate.

They currently use their grapes for their winery and also sell tonnage to Arterberry-Maresh and Winderlea.

"When we moved here in 1987 people told us we were to late, we had missed the curve in the rise of the industry," said Julia.

The name of the winery, Crumbled Rock, refers to the hillside Jory soil and underlying deeply weathered basalt, an ancient iron-rich volcanic basalt that has weathered in place and is a perfect medium for growing pinot noir grapes.

Julia often explains to customers in the tasting room that operating a vineyard and operating a winery are two completely different things.

"The vineyard and winery are like a farmer and a baker. The farmer grows the wheat and the baker bakes the bread. They are two inherently different processes but connected by the same product, grapes," said Julia.

Tom and Sharon Saucy:
Saucy Vineyards

The Saucy's bought ten acres in the Dundee Hills in 1971. They built a house and planted a nine-acre vineyard over the next five years. They sold the house and vineyard to Julia Staigers and Gerard Koschal in 1987, who named it Juliard Vineyards.

"We were crazy people, I don't really know how we did it, but we did," said Sharon Saucy, recalling the years of building a house and planting a vineyard.

The Saucy's decided to buy vineyard property in Dundee in 1971 after a few forays into other winemaking areas. Initially, they thought of winemaking in Switzerland, where Tom was a first-generation Swiss citizen.

During this time, Tom, a mechanical engineer at Tektronix, took a winemaking class and started making fruit wine in the living room. He fermented the fruit wine in glass carboys, where they bubbled away amidst family life. Dick Erath and Ron Vulsteke of Oak Knoll also worked at Tektronix.

The Saucy's also traveled to Napa Valley and watched the harvest, and belonged to an amateur winemaking club in Beaverton that included the Vulsteke's who established Oak Knoll.

After they bought the vineyard property, the family continued to live in Cedar Hills. During that time, they planted the vineyard and remodeled an existing cottage on the property.

Sharon recalled one morning when a truck from Wente Nursery from California showed up with 10,000 cuttings at their Cedar Mills home. The deliveryman asked where he she was going to put them.

She joked, "Oh, I'm going to plant them in the front and back lawn."

Instead, they planted the cuttings behind Tom's father's house in Dundee, and bought a twenty-year-old tractor to clear the land.

Their first planting was Gewurztraminer. They eventually planted Pinot noir, Chardonnay, Riesling and a few Cabernet sauvignon plants.

They sold their harvested grapes to Erath and Oak Knoll until they sold the property in 1987

"People think it's this big romantic adventure. In reality, it's really a big job," said Sharon.

Dick and Kina Erath:
Knudsen-Erath Winery,
Currently Erath Winery/Chateau St. Michelle.

Dick Erath and his former wife Kina Erath moved to Oregon in 1968. His career is chronicled in the "Boys up North" by Paul Pintarich. Rob Stuart of R. Stuart and Co. worked at the winery for several years before he started his own winery with his wife Maria.

Dick Erath was in the electronics business in San Francisco for fifteen years before he decided he needed a change. After a brief interlude with three acres of vineyard in Walnut Creek, he decided to come north and make his way in the Oregon wine industry.

Although Erath's father, Charles, was a German immigrant and a trained cooper (barrel-maker), Dick was an engineer by trade. By nature an intellectually curious man, he was intrigued with the world of wine.

Knudsen-Erath White Riesling Label, 1977.

Erath came to Oregon in 1968 and worked for Tektronix in Beaverton. He met both Richard Somers and Charles Coury, who helped him with his first rootstock. He bought his first vineyard that year, Chehalem Mountain Vineyards, a forty-nine acre site located on Dopp Road in the Chehalem Mountains above Newberg.

In 1971, he quit Tektronix and devoted himself full-time to winemaking. His first vintage was in 1971, when he made primarily Gewürztraminer and Riesling, with a small amount of Pinot noir. At the time, sweet, white wine was popular with the public, and sold well. He continued to produce wine and refine his winemaking technique on his own.

During this time, he marketed wine to local stores and abroad in California. He began to gain recognition, and win awards for his vintages. In 1979 he won a prestigious award at a winemaking competition in France for his 1976 Pinot noir.

In 1975 Erath and C. Calvert Knudsen, a wine-enthusiast and former vice-president of Weyerhaeuser, formed the Knudsen Erath partnership that would last until the mid 1980s. (Knudsen went on to form Argyle winery partnership in 1985). Knudsen bought a two-hundred acre parcel in the Red Hills for their future winery. Knudsen was the financial manager; Dick was the official winemaker and general manager of the vineyards.

Dick Erath continues to operate the former Knudsen-Erath winery under the 'Erath' name in the original tasting room and winery. He bought his grapes from local vineyards, and grows his own on his housing site.

The winery tasting room, with its panoramic view of the valley and local history, is a popular tourist destination. The winery is one of the longest-running, successful wineries in Oregon today.

Jim Maresh and Dick Erath, Dundee Hills, 1979.

Cal Erath, Dundee Hills, 1979.

Alan and Holstein:

Holstein Vineyards

Alan Holstein came to Oregon in 1980 and worked for Knudsen-Erath winery as a vineyard manager. He bought one of Gary Fuqua's vineyards in the early 1980s. He is currently the vineyard manager for Argyle.

Alan Holstein came to Oregon in 1980 to work on a Ph. D in horticulture at Oregon State University. During Christmas of 1979, he also visited the tasting room at Knudsen-Erath winery on his way to the airport. That day, he met Dick and Kina Erath, and said he was from the horticulture department at OSU.

"Good," said Kina Erath, "I'm looking for a vineyard manager."

Holstein answered, "I'll do it."

Kina replied, "Well, I mean someone who has some experience."

Holstein convinced the couple that he could do the job - and got hired.

He joined a small group of full-time vineyard managers scattered around the state, a group that included Rich Cushman, Mark Benoit and Joey Maresh. He remains the only one of the group to have consistently managed an Oregon vineyard for the last 23 years.

Like many others who moved to the hills, he lived in the Knudsen cabin before he purchased his vineyard land.

"It was catch as catch can - a very bohemian lifestyle," said Holstein.

Holstein has been interested in wine ever since he and college roommate, Ken Wright, lived in San Francisco in the late 1970s. Ken worked at a restaurant. Together, they started tasting different wines on the list, which included Beaujolais, Burgundy and Spanish wines.

They both were bitten by the wine bug. Wright went to UC Davis to study winemaking, and Holstein went on to OSU for his PhD. work.

Ken would eventually become an accomplished Oregon winemaker. He founded Panther Creek Winery in McMinnville and then established Ken Wright Cellars in Carlton. In 2015 he was featured on the cover of The Wine Spectator magazine.

When Holstein started work at Knudsen-Erath in 1980, grapes starts were fifty cents a plant. He remembers that vineyards were planted with approximately five-hundred plants per acre. In 2003, starts cost three dollars a plant and he plants rows of up to three-thousand plants per acre.

He also remembers harvesting six tons per acre at Knudsen-Erath in the early 1980s, three tons more per acre than the winemaker wanted. His recollection is a sharp contrast to the high-density, low yield vineyard planting techniques and management he practices at Argyle Winery today.

Holstein has seen the evolution of the Oregon wine industry from it's humble beginnings to it's well-acclaimed success today. Among Argyle's fans are former president Bill Clinton, who ordered Argyle sparkling wine for a dinner in the 1990s. Winemaker Rollin Soles is educated at Davis, and made wine in Australia before he and others formed Argyle.

Ken Wright and Alan Holstein, McDaniel Vineyards, 1984.

Holstein and Soles had a close working relationship for years before Soles left Argyle to start his current winery, Roco. Together, they pushed the boundaries of innovative and successful winemaking and grape growing.

There is a synergism between the two managers; a unique relationship not always found in the wine industry. In France, there is no word for vineyard manager. The manager is as essential as the winemaker in the winemaking process. The French believe that a quality bottle of wine begins with quality fruit. Holstein has made a career out of studying and implementing the most effective vineyard management techniques, many of which he's learned by traveling to France.

Historically, Europeans, including the French, Germans and Italians, have been making wine for, well, a long time, longer than any Oregon winemakers. Holstein thought he could learn a thing or two from their experience, and that hasn't always made him popular with proponents of 'the way it's always been done' in Oregon.

"The bohemian element is still here, but French vineyard growing techniques really revolutionized the system," said Holstein.

From his studies, he's convinced that high-density low yield technique is the most effective way to produce world-class vinifera.

On a crisp fall day we drive through the vineyard rows on the original planting site of Knudsen-Erath winery. We drive by some of the first plantings which were planted before the modern catch wire system. The bushy rows were a pruning and tying nightmare.

His job is different now. He operates Argyle's vineyard management company, which is composed of five-hundred acres and four vineyard sites.

In the early days, the 'intercom' system at Knudsen-Erath for announcing a phone call was to shoot a flare gun out the window. Now he communicates by cell phone with his workers, some of whom work in the vineyards year-round. He used to communicate by walkie talkie, or just plain walking.

Holstein has also seen the evolution of winemaking through changing harvesting approaches. Winemaker's used to just pick for brix, as high as you could get them, during chilly Oregon falls. Now they winemaker pick for taste, as well as brix. Holstein says Soles can taste a grape and tell if it's ready to be picked or not, without using a refractometer. These growing techniques have changed the quality of wine, and grafting has changed the quality of the vines.

The quality of winemaking has been elevated, too. Wine would occasionally turn blue for no reason, and entire vintages could be lost to experimental technique gone awry.

A cacophony of bird screeches echo through the vineyard. Argyle installed advanced bird sound systems in the more recent vineyard plantings. This technology is a sharp contrast to the shotgun Holstein carried as he rode around on a three-wheeler ATV scaring birds.

When he started in 1980, he managed the sixty-six acres of Knudsen-Erath and thirty-three acres of Erath's Chehalem Vineyard off Dopp Road north of Newberg. His official title was 'vineyard foreman'. He went back and forth to both vineyards and off and on the tractor several times a day. In general, he remembers doing less supervising and more 'getting down in the trenches' with the help.

Although he had five or six people helping throughout the year, a number that grew briefly for the harvest crew - he now manages a vineyard crew of seventy with middle management help.

"I was a wild man back then. I worked like crazy, all the time, just to keep the vineyard operating," recalled Holstein.

Lion Corporation in Australia now owns Argyle and the current winemaker is Nate Klostermann.

Pamphlet cover for Charles Coury Nursery, 1974

Charles and Shirley Coury:
Coury Winery, Vineyards and Nursery

The Coury's bought forty-five acres with an abandoned vineyard on Rueter Hill, also known as David Hill, near Forest Grove in 1965. They operated a winery, vineyard and nursery until 1978. Coury planted twenty-five acres of Pinot noir and Chardonnay vineyards. The site became Laurel Ridge Winery, and is currently David Hill Winery. His sister-in-law, Betts Coury, helped establish the winery.

"He was ahead of his time," said Betts Coury, Charles Coury's sister in law, (Charles is known to the family as Chuck.) "He had all the right ideas about how to start a winery in Oregon - and he proved it could be done."

The Coury's also started the first microbrewery in Oregon - Cartwright Brewing, in the late 1970s.

The roots of the Oregon wine industry can be traced to Coury's early years in California, when he lived in Laguna Beach in the mid 1950s. He sold liquor for Julius Wile Distributing, and learned to love the German wines they distributed. He was a top salesman, and was sent often to L.A. for tastings, where he learned more about wine and met some of the top names in the burgeoning Napa wine industry.

Chuck and Shirley, a registered nurse, often came to visit Betts and Coury's brother Ron, whom she married in 1965. Betts lived in Alamo, a suburb of the Bay area and close to Napa Valley. They often drank wine and explored the wine region together.

During that time, Betts belonged to a wine group that included an array of people who would later establish significant wineries in both California and Oregon. Betts went on to help form Coury Vineyards, members Bill and Virginia Fuller would later go to UC Davis and establish another pioneer Oregon winery he named Tualatin Vineyards. Jack and Jamie Davies became owners of Schramsberg winery in Napa. The Wisnovsky, other members, founded Stag's Leap in Napa.

Chuck was intrigued with the idea of being a winemaker. He already had a degree from the University of California at Los Angeles in climatology. He understood growing seasons, and the cyclical nature of agriculture. He enrolled and UC Davis in the early 1960s to study viticulture and started his journey towards Oregon winemaking.

"The reason I moved to Oregon in 1965 was to prove that excellent Burgundian and Alsatian wine grapes could be grown there. California certainly wasn't producing any decent Pinot noir. For that matter, no one at the time in any other part of the United States could really produce a decent Pinot," recalled Chuck in a 2004 phone conversation. "But anyway, those guys in California just couldn't produce a decent pinot, but I could, so I did."

Immortalized in Oregon wine lore for his opinionated observations and dramatic style, Coury still enjoys his status as the self-proclaimed 'second person to make a decent wine in Oregon.' Second, he says to Richard Sommers, of Hillcrest Winery in Roseburg, who started making wine in 1961.

"Sommers is the original pioneer, not me. But I was the second. Before Lett, before Fuller, before Erath. I graduated way ahead of those guys. Heck, they all read my thesis at Davis on cold-climate growing and argued with me about if it could be done successfully in Oregon," said Coury.

Coury described his long debates in the student union with Lett and Fuller, as they sat and debated the pros and cons of wine growing in the region; and as Coury described, 'listened to his rhetoric.'

Coury said that most students at the time wanted to make money in the already established California wine business.

"I guess my opinions must have been persuasive, because a few years later they all showed up in Oregon," he said.

After graduating from Davis with a Masters degree in viticulture, he was awarded a prestigious scholarship to study wine at the Alsace Wine Research Station in Colmar. He went for the year and returned in 1965. His experience at the station, which had a climate very similar to the one in Oregon, confirmed his opinions.

Years later, his son, Charlie, who spoke fluent French, would receive the exact same scholarship.

Coury's arrival in Oregon may confirm that he was, if not the first, the second after Richard Sommers and before David Lett, according to Betts.

"David and Chuck would get into it about Alsace and David would tell him he was nuts. David got converted to the idea of growing grapes in Oregon when he went to visit Chuck in Alsace," said Betts.

Coury came to Oregon with his father and bought his vineyard site in 1965, on a former winery site in Forest Grove.

The Coury's bought the acreage for thirty-six thousand, a figure that priced the one-hundred year-old farmhouse on the property as nearly valueless. They moved into the house with their two young sons, Brad and Charlie.

Farmers who had previously farmed the land had grown potatoes in the basement. There were holes in the floor and visquine over the windows. It was more of a greenhouse than a home.

"Everyone lived in some sort of cabin during those years. They did what they had to do to make their dream come true," said Betts.

Betts and Shirley drove the 45-minute drive to the Sellwood antique district in Portland to refurbish the decrepit farmhouse.

"Shirley was always up for Chuck's grand adventures. She really supported him in many ways. She believed in him," remembered Betts.

Chuck planted additional acreage in Pinot noir, Chardonnay, Gewürztraminer and Riesling. He hired a young winemaker named Richard Wirtz.

Here is where urban myth contrasts with the truth.

"I did bring root stock back from Alsace. It was called the Bergheimer clone, and I brought it in my suitcase," said Chuck. This clone would eventually be called the Coury Clone, and he would win an award for it in Napa thirty years later.

However, he also shipped cuttings to the agricultural quarantine port in San Francisco, where he picked them up and drove them up to Oregon.

He formed a nursery with a greenhouse on the land, where he propagated root stock for growers. He established a large operation quickly, which strained the demands of growers who needed more root stock than he could provide.

"He dreamed big dreams," said Betts.

Coury's ideas about Oregon wine proved correct. Where virtually no Oregon wine market existed in 1973, Coury's salesperson, Betts, established accounts with Fred Meyer, Stroheckers, Elephant Deli, Wizers and Grape n' Grain in Eugene.

"The message I got from the distributors was 'Oregon is a beer drinking state, not a wine drinking state.' So we were the distributors at that point. There was Henny-Hinsdale, Giusti, and some other big names, but no one really believed in Oregon wine at that point," recalled Betts.

Betts worked hard getting Coury wine on the shelves, where she battled for space amidst a few Oregon wines and imported German and California wines.

"I finally got six spaces for my wine on the shelf at Fred Meyer. I came back a week later, and someone had moved it off the shelf to the back room and replaced the spaces with imported wine," recalled Betts.

They also sold the wine in restaurants, including Henry Theiles and L'Omelette, where a young sommelier named David Adelsheim worked. Adelsheim would eventually form Adelsheim Vineyards with his wife, Ginny.

"I'd back up to the winery and load my 1973 Volvo up with wine. Then I'd drive off to sell wine in the Portland area for the day. The problem was, I was from California and didn't know my way around very well," laughed Betts.

The Coury Winery produced Pinot noir, Chardonnay, Gewürztraminer and Zwicker, a blended white table wine.

Unfortunately, for financial reasons, the Coury winery only survived for thirteen, albeit dynamic, years.

"I figured it'd take about fifteen years to develop a decent industry. It killed me emotionally (his decision to sell the winery in 1978). By '78, I realized that the wines were good; they had also started to sell at a decent pace in the restaurant and grocery industry. I knew I had started something that was so much bigger than anyone could have imagined," said Chuck.

Yamhill County Wine Industry Information

There are seven major towns in Yamhill County - McMinnville, Dundee, Newberg, Dayton, Carlton, Yamhill and Sheridan. Each city offers a variety of unique dining, lodging and wine tasting options.

Dundee Hills Winegrowers Association:
This website features a comprehensive list of wine industry growers, vintners and business owners.
wwwdundeehills.org

Newberg Chamber of Commerce and Visitors Center:
The Chamber website offers a useful local business directory website of business to search for lodging, wineries, restaurant and information.
www.chehalemvalley.org

McMinnville Chamber of Commerce and Visitors Center: Detailed listings for McMinnville AVA.
www.mcminnvillechamber.org

Willamette Valley Wineries Association:
This is a great resource for larger tours throughout the Willamette Valley. They have a comprehensive listing of all vineyards and wineries with a brochure that can be found in tasting rooms.
www.willamettewines.com

Oregon Wine Board:
The Wine Board is the oldest, most comprehensive resource for wineries, touring and events throughout Oregon.
www.oregonwine.org

International Pinot Noir Conference: This event is a three day celebration of Pinot Noir at historic Linfield College Campus in McMinnville, complete with an annual salmon bake in the oak grove.
www.ipnc.org

Oregon Chardonnay Symposium: This annual event focuses on all aspects of growing, making and tasting chardonnay, with technical seminars by industry experts and a spectacular Chardonnay tasting session.
www.oregonchardonnaysymposium.com

Oregon Riesling Alliance: This is a listing of Oregon riesling producers.
www.oregonriesling.org

Oregon Truffle Festival: This annual event is held in Yamhill County and Eugene, Oregon and features an incredible array of truffle food, truffle chefs and industry speakers.
www.oregontrufflefestival.com

Wineries in the Dundee Hills AVA

Alexana Winery
Anderson Family Vineyard
Archery Summit
Argyle Winery
Armonéa Vineyard & Winery
Arterberry Maresh Red Barn Tasting Room
Ayoub Winery
Barrel Fence Cellars
Bella Vida Vineyard
Black Walnut Vineyard
Crumbled Rock Winery
DePonte Cellars
Dobbes Family Estate
Domaine Drouhin
Domaine Serene
Domaine Trouvère
Durant Vineyards
Dusky Goose
Élevée Winegrowers
Erath Winery
Fox Farm Vineyards
Hyland Estates
Lange Estate Winery & Vineyards
Native Flora
NW Wine Company
Nysa Vineyard
Panther Creek Cellars
Purple Hands Winery
ROCO Winery
Sokol Blosser Winery
Stoller Family Estate
The Four Graces
Thistle Wines
Torii Mor Vineyard & Winery
Tractor and Vine

Vista Hills Vineyard & Winery
White Rose Estate
Winderlea Vineyard & Winery
Winter's Hill Vineyard

Vineyards
Baptista Maresh Vineyard
Domaine Roy
DUX Vineyard
Knudsen Vineyards
Lillie's Vineyard
Murto Vineyard
Overlook Vineyard
Renton Family Vineyard
Terrarossa Vineyard
Wilson Fjord Vineyard

Places to stay in Dundee area:
Black Walnut Inn
Distinctive Destinations
Dundee Manor Bed & Breakfast
Franziska Haus Bed and Breakfast
Le Puy A Wine Valley Inn
Maresh Red Hills Vineyard Retreat
Red Ridge Farm Apartment
Stoller Guest Houses
The Inn at Red Hills
Wine Country Farm B&B

Restaurants in Dundee:

Tina's: www.tinasdundee.com
This restaurant has been open since 1991 for a good reason, Tina is still cooking locally sourced meat, seafood and vegetables in the kitchen. The menu changes weekly. White table clothes, an extensive wine list and a fireplace contribute to the cozy atmosphere.

Red Hills Market: www.redhillsmarket.com
Red Hills market features local products chosen by owners Michelle and Jody Kropf. A great place for coffee pastries and quiche in the deli case for breakfast. For lunch and dinner the casual wine country setting features a wide selection of cheeses, charcuterie, craft beer and wine.
They can also prepare picnics, lunch to go and wood fired pizza.

Ponzi Bistro: www.dundeebistro.com
From the website: "On a given day it's possible to order handmade pizza, fish and chips, salad of mixed organic greens with seared foie gras, Kumamoto oysters fresh from the Pacific 60 miles away, roasted butternut squash soup with chanterelles, loin of venison or local, natural pork smoked all day over local walnut to tender perfection. The wine program for The Dundee Bistro, under the guidance of the Ponzi Family, offers emphasis on local Pinot Noirs, rare vintages and bottlings, as well as an award-winning international selection of the world's finest producers."

Red Hills Provincial Restaurant: www.redhills-dining.com
Owner's Richard and Nancy Gehrts serve locally sourced food in a charming restored Craftsman home with a fireplace and dark fir trim work. They use organic herbs and vegetables grown in their organic garden and cook from a four generation family cookbook of recipes.

Bert's Chuckwagon: www.bertschuckwagon.com
Bert's is the best BBQ in Dundee. Ribs, pulled pork sandwiches, fries, tots and onion rings to go with all the traditional side dishes. Patio seating and heat lamps add to the ambience. Open seven days a week from 11:00 a.m. to 8:00 p.m.

Chan's Chinese Restaurant: www.chansofdundee.com

The owner's of Chan's offer a wide assortment of traditional Chinese dishes from Peking, Mongolian, Hunan, Shanghai and Cantonese providences cooked without MSG. They are open seven days a week and offer a lunch special.

La Sierra Restaurant: www.sierramexicanrestaurant.com

This is a great family moderately priced restaurant in a newly expanded space.

Babica Hen: www.babicahencafe.com

As their website says, "We are passionate about good food, and we love cooking it for you. Our eggs are local and farm fresh as is the pasture raised pork and all-natural beef. Our baked goods are prepared from scratch in house and our sausage, batters, sauces all house made.

Lumpy's Tavern: 503-538-9719/facebook: Lumpy's

Lumpy's has an impressive selection of beer on tap and an ambience like no other tavern in the county. Live music on weekends. An amazing huge burger and vodka jello shots make this tavern an unforgettable adventure in wine country.

Road tour #1: The Pioneer Trail - Worden Hill/ Fairview Road loop

This pioneer trail day tour starts with Argyle in downtown Dundee. The rest of the tour can be done in a three mile radius by driving two blocks south of Argyle on highway 99W and turning on 9th street to access all tasting rooms on the loop in the order that they are listed. Along the way enjoy scenery with stunning views of Mt. Hood and old growth vineyards. There are a multitude of lunch and dinner options in Dundee. Watching movies outdoors at the historic 99w drive in Newberg is a great way to end this tour during the summer. Argyle, Crumbled Rock, Barrel Fence, Winderlea, Erath, Alexana, Lange, Torii Mor and Cameron (open only holiday weekends).

Road Tour #2: 99W/The Straight Shot to Oregon Coast

This tour begins on at A to Z in Newberg on Highway 99w. It ends in McMinnville on the way to the beach. Lunch in Newberg at Storr's BBQ. Dine in McMinnville for dinner on the rooftop of McMennamins Hotel, which is within blocks of R. Stuart and Eyrie. The beach at Lincoln City is an hour from downtown McMinnville on Highway 47. Stay at the Vintages Trailer Resort halfway between Dundee and Dayton for added fun. www.the-vintages.com
A to Z/Rex Hill, Hyland Estates, Stoller, R. Stuart and Eyrie.

Road Tour #3: Dayton Chateaus and Vistas:

This tour begins at Archery Summit located aptly on Archery Summit Road off of Hwy 99w. Sokol-Blosser is the second stop on this tour, which features a diverse mix of old growth pinot noir, organic wines and an interesting affordable blend called Evolution. The third and fourth wineries are straight up the hill a mile and from both there are stunning almost 360 degree vistas. Dine in Dayton
at the Barlow Trail Restaurant or Martha's Tacos in Lafayette, where the industry locals often go for authentic hand rolled tortillas baked in the kitchen by Martha.

If you want to go upscale, try the Joel Palmer House in Dayton which features truffles in almost every dish and an extensive Pinot Noir wine list. Spend the night at the Vintages Trailer Resort in Dayton.
Archery summit, Sokol-Blosser, Domaine Drouhin, Domaine Serene, White Rose.

Road Tour #4: Historic Carlton/Yamhill

Start in Carlton. Bring your swimming suit and take a dip during the summer in the outdoor Carlton Pool. Common Grounds Espresso is a good picnic option for fresh delicious deli sandwiches. Cielo Blu is open for lunch is a casual bistro setting. Cuvee Italian restaurant is a dinner favorite with an extensive wine list. Wind through the countryside to Saffron Fields and conclude with Elk Cove Vineyards in Gaston, which features fantastic old-growth vines and a beautiful pastoral setting amidst the oak trees.
Ken Wright, Carlton Winemaker's Studio, Saffron Fields and Elk Cove Winery.

Oregon AVA listings

There are nine American Viticultural Associations (AVA) in Oregon. They each have their own website that includes tour information, maps and comprehensive listings of the specific AVA wineries:

Chehalem Mountains
www.chehalemmountains.org

Ribbon Ridge
www.chehalemmountains.org

Dundee Hills
www.dundeehills.org

Yamhill-Carlton
www.yamhillcarlton.org

McMinnville
www.mcminnvilleava.org

Eola-Amity Hills
www.eolaamityhills.com

South Willamette Valley
www.oregonpinotnoirwine.com

Umpqua Valley
www.umpquavalleywineries.org

Columbia Gorge
www.columbiagorgewineries.com

About the Author:

Kerry McDaniel Boenisch has a degree in English from the University of Oregon and grew up on McDaniel Vineyards, now Torii Mor Winery.

She wrote the book Vineyard Memoirs in 2004. Dirt+Vine=Wine is her second publication. She is currently writing a third book, Fall Down, Stand Up, about the art of transcending loss and making comebacks.

In her other lives, she has been a photostylist for commercial television and movie sets, operated a vintage furniture store and worked for Knoll Textiles in New York City.

She and her husband have three children and live on a farm in Dundee, where they attended grade school together.

Her website is www.kerrymcdanielboenisch.com and dirtvinewine.com

Wine Journal

WINERY VISITED: _____

WINERY VISITED: _____

WINERY VISITED: _____

WINERY VISITED: _____

WINERY VISITED: _____

WINERY VISITED: _____

WINERY VISITED: _____

WINERY VISITED: _____

WINERY VISITED: _____

WINERY VISITED: _____

WINERY VISITED: _____

WINERY VISITED: _____

WINERY VISITED: _____

WINERY VISITED: _____

WINERY VISITED: _____

WINERY VISITED: _____

WINERY VISITED: _____

WINERY VISITED: _____

WINERY VISITED: _____

WINERY VISITED: _____

WINERY VISITED: _____

WINERY VISITED: _____

WINERY VISITED: _____

WINERY VISITED: _____

WINERY VISITED: _____

WINERY VISITED: _____

WINERY VISITED: _____

WINERY VISITED: _____

WINERY VISITED: _____

WINERY VISITED: _____

NOTES:

NOTES:

NOTES:

NOTES:

NOTES:

NOTES:

NOTES:

NOTES:

NOTES:

NOTES:

NOTES:

NOTES:

NOTES:

NOTES:

NOTES:

NOTES:

NOTES:

NOTES:

NOTES:

115

NOTES:

NOTES:

NOTES:

NOTES:

NOTES:

NOTES:

NOTES:

NOTES:

NOTES:

NOTES:

NOTES:

NOTES:

NOTES:

NOTES:

NOTES:

NOTES:

NOTES:

NOTES:

NOTES:

NOTES:

Made in the USA
Middletown, DE
13 January 2019